# Learn to Have Fun with Your SENSES

## The Sensory Avoider's Survival Guide

**John Taylor, PhD**

Illustrations by Lynda Farrington Wilson

Sensory World / Arlington, TX
*www.SensoryWorld.com*

Learn to Have Fun with Your Senses:
The Sensory Avoider's Survival Guide

A proud imprint of Future Horizons

Sensory World
info@sensoryworld.com
www.sensoryworld.com
(877) 775-8968
(682) 558-8941
(682) 558-8945 (fax)

Cover and interior design © TLC Graphics, www.TLCGraphics.com
Cover by: Monica Thomas / Interior by: Tamara Dever

ISBN: 978-1-935567-24-0

TO TAMMY, BRIAN, DANA, BETH,
SHARON, JOHN, AMY AND MICHAEL,
AND TO JEANIE.

# TABLE of CONTENTS

# TABLE of CONTENTS continued

# A SPECIAL MESSAGE
# for the Parent

*This book represents an introduction* to the human senses. It might be your child's first "read about your own problems" guide. It explains what can go wrong when the brain inappropriately magnifies the messages sense organs send to it.

There are three categories of abnormal sensory response: underresponding to senses, excessive seeking of sensory stimulation, and excessive avoidance of sensory stimulation. This book is basically a therapy guide for any child who exhibits the third category of abnormality and overly avoids sensory messages. The child avoids, resists, or becomes emotionally upset about experiencing sensory awareness, to a level that significantly interferes with a child's ability to perform the necessary major functions of daily living.

Children with major distortions of how their brains "read" the messages from their sense organs usually have one or more psychiatric conditions or diagnoses. I have avoided discussion of those specific diagnostic categories and have kept the book general, so it can be applied to your child without conflicting with any other medical or psychiatric topics.

There are very few books that invite a child to "ask your parent to..." This is one of those books. Without the insights in this book, your child might conclude that the best explanation for his or her overreactions to senses is that he or she is weird, lazy, or stupid. Please maintain an open channel of communication, answering the sincere questions that will no doubt emerge when your child reads this book.

The therapeutic sensory experiences that an occupational therapist would recommend are intended primarily to gradually desensitize your child to sensory messages from a specific sense. This book facilitates that process by describing commonly recommended interventions that are delightfully pleasant ways your child can gradually become desensitized and stop overreacting. It helps your child understand how important and helpful these activities can be. It shows your child exactly how to cooperate fully to get maximum advantage and benefit from the activities.

Doing the delightful activities in this book is not the whole story, however. To decrease any child's overreaction to sensory messages, it is important to ensure sufficient sleep, adequate brain nutrition, stress relief, and avoidance of toxic chemical exposures that could interfere with the brain's functioning.

In 2008, the American Academy of Pediatrics (AAP) reversed a long-standing trend to dismiss the overwhelming amount of documented scientific evidence about the risk of symptom flare-ups due to toxic chemical exposures, especially in children with attention-deficit disorder and autism spectrum disorders. Whereas there have been more than 400 such studies conducted over the past 40 years, the AAP had consistently claimed that the evidence was insufficient to justify advising parents to reduce toxic chemical exposures to their children. This dramatic formal announcement by the AAP supports the use of a preservative-free and dye-free diet (actually not a diet but a program of toxic-chemical insulation) for these children as a legitimate intervention for reducing their symptoms. The AAP was responding to a landmark study involving 300 children that was exceptionally well designed in terms of its scientific rigor, which found that additives caused hyperactivity in both young and older children.

Writing about that study in the February 2008 official publication of the AAP, called "AAP Grand Rounds," Alison Schonwald noted that additional support for the benefits of an additive-free diet came from a then-current meta-analysis of 15 additional scientific studies that found evidence linking a wide range of "chemicals" to "neurobehavioral toxicity." Schonwald concluded that the evidence indicates that for many children (especially those with attention-deficit disorder and autism spectrum disorders), "a trial of a preservative-free, food coloring–free diet is a reasonable intervention."

The editors of "AAP Grand Rounds" added that "...we skeptics, who have long doubted parental claims of the effects of various foods on the behavior of their children, admit we might have been wrong."

I have therefore included some helpful references to guide you in adding this approach to whatever else you are doing to assist your child. With the blessings of an official endorsement from the AAP, your diligent attempt to insulate your child from toxic chemical exposures through common food additives may be met with much more enthusiasm by the members of your child's team than would have been the case in prior years. I introduce this issue briefly to your child in chapter 8. There are additional sources of toxic chemical exposure besides food additives, and addressing those other sources of brain upset can also help your child. I've offered some suggestions to guide you in the Resources section.

This book invites your child to come to you and talk about nutrition, sleep, stress, and the suggested activities. My intention is that this book will provide a bridge to help bring you closer to your child, emotionally and physically. Also, it should open important doors for successful treatment and improve self-care with respect to your child's sensory-avoidance symptoms.

# Learn to Have Fun with Your Senses

*Your brain is the boss of your body.* It tells your muscles what to do. But before it can decide what position to put your body in, or where you should walk or run to, it has to know what is happening in the world around you. That's what your senses do. They send messages to your brain, telling it what is happening around you, so your brain can figure out what to tell your muscles to do.

## YOUR SENSES AND YOUR BRAIN ARE PALS

Your brain and your sense organs—your eyes, ears, nose, tongue, and skin—work together to make sure that you are safe. They also help you make the body movements you need to survive and to enjoy your life. If the air is cold outside, your brain reminds you to put

*"Your brain and your sense organs —your eyes, ears, nose, tongue, and skin—work together to make sure that you are safe."*

on a coat before going outside. But how does it know if it's cold outside? With your eyes, you use your *sense of vision* to read the thermometer, so your brain knows what the temperature is. By sticking your hand out a slightly open door for a few seconds, you use your *sense of touch* to feel what the air is like outside. With your ears, your *sense of hearing,* you can listen to the weather forecast on the radio.

## What Overreacting Means

But what if something goes wrong with how your brain "reads" the messages it gets from your sense organs? What if it reacts TOO much? Then a fluorescent light in the ceiling at school that appears somewhat bright to most other kids seems TERRIBLY bright. Clothes made of fabric that seems smooth to

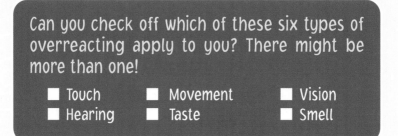

Can you check off which of these six types of overreacting apply to you? There might be more than one!

■ Touch    ■ Movement    ■ Vision
■ Hearing    ■ Taste    ■ Smell

most kids feel TERRIBLY rough or TERRIBLY ticklish. In a stadium, a referee's whistle that most kids could ignore seems TERRIBLY loud. Going down a slide on the playground seems TERRIBLY fast!

## What Overreacting Does NOT Mean

Overreacting to what your senses feel doesn't mean that something is wrong with your sense organs. It means that something is going wrong in how your brain *handles* the messages it receives from your sense organs. Overreacting to a sound doesn't mean that your ears aren't working right. It means that your brain is magnifying the messages it's receiving from your ears!

So overreacting to your senses means that something is going wrong inside your brain. The billions of cells in your brain are not handling the messages well. It does *not* mean that you are crazy, stupid, or lazy. And it does *not* mean that there are germs or dirt in your brain. Your brain is not sick or dying! It handles *most* of the messages from your sense organs okay, but not *all* of them. This collection of a few messages that it magnifies ends up causing you to overreact.

*"Overreacting is more likely to happen when your **brain** doesn't get enough of what it needs."*

## WHAT YOUR BRAIN NEEDS

Overreacting is more likely to happen when your brain doesn't get enough of what it needs. Your brain needs three things every day: *(1)* "brain food" (which we'll talk about in chapter 7), *(2)* enough sleep, and *(3)* not having too many chemicals sent into it. Some glands in your body send chemicals into your body and brain when you are under too much stress. Other chemicals can get into your brain from outside your body, such as when you eat food that has chemicals added to it. If your brain gets more of the three things it needs, it can do a better job of handling the messages from your senses. If it *doesn't* get enough of these three things, it is more likely to have problems and overreact.

# THE ANSWER IS TO USE YOUR SENSES

This book is about helping you learn to have fun with your senses—touch, movement, vision, hearing, taste, and smell. When you overreact to what your senses tell you, things don't feel pleasant and safe. They feel very unpleasant, confusing, and unsafe to touch, hear, look at, taste, or smell. Anything to do with your senses has a special name: "sensory."

*Trying to stop using your senses is NOT the answer.* Going through life always afraid to touch, hear, or taste things that others touch, listen to, and taste is also NOT the answer. The answer is to go ahead and use your senses, but in special ways. This book will help you learn the ways to use your senses so that they slowly start to feel better to you over time. Throughout this book, you will see sections called, "Train Your Brain!" These sections are about activities you can do at home, at school, and when you are out in public to train your brain to stop being overly aware of what your senses do. If you do these activities, you will be able to reduce—or maybe even totally stop—the overreacting. So let's get to it!

# HOW TO USE THIS BOOK

Each of your senses is introduced with a little quiz, to find out whether you overreact to that sense. If you overreact to that sense, you should read that chapter. It is okay to read the other chapters, even though they might not apply to you.

There are all kinds of families. In this book, a "parent" means an adult who lives with you and cares for you. Sometimes other adults might be helping you. One of those people might have special training in how to help children control body parts, muscles, and senses. This person has a title of "occupational therapist," often with "OT" as a nickname.

Show the lists of activities to your parent or to an OT who is helping you. Point out the ones you want to try. They all help you learn to have fun with your senses. In fact, they're SO MUCH fun that you'll probably want to try them, even if you don't overreact to the senses involved in them!

Some of the activities involve asking your parent or teacher to help you. Always listen to the advice of your parent and any other adult who is assisting in your care, such as an OT, about which activities to do. Even if it sounds like fun, if your parent or OT says it's not the best for you, then don't try it.

*"always listen to the advice of your parent and any other adult who is assisting in your care, such as an OT, about which activities to do."*

# CHAPTER 2

# Stop Overreacting in Three Steps

*There are three important steps* you need to do to help train your brain and body to stop overreacting.

### STEP 1
Do some activities every day, or as often as your OT says.

### STEP 2
Tell your parent and OT about the changes you notice.

### STEP 3
Give your brain good nutrition, enough sleep, and protection from stress chemicals every day.

This chapter explains Step 1, the activities you can do to help train your brain to stop over-reacting, and Step 2, how to tell your parent and OT about the changes you notice.

The last three chapters in this book explain Step 3, how to give your brain more nutrition, more sleep, and more protection from stress chemicals and outside chemicals. Be sure to read these chapters and try your best to do everything they say. Maybe you can discuss them with your parent and OT, and have them read the book along with you!

## STEP 1: DO YOUR ACTIVITIES

The activities suggested here, and the ones your OT will suggest for you, are special. They are special because they are also:

- FUN. Many are games you can play, to learn new ways to experience your senses. They are often great to do with a friend or your brother or sister!

- SHORTCUTS. Doing the activities will speed up the process of learning to not overreact. The more of them you do, and the more often, the faster your brain and body will learn to stop overreacting.

- CONVENIENT. Some of them you can do almost anywhere and at almost any time!

- PLEASING. Learning to avoid overreacting will feel much better to you. Some of these activities will also make your parent and teacher happy, and some will make your friends, classmates, and brothers and sisters happier too!

- ENJOYABLE. You will probably want to do some of these activities for years and years, just because they feel so good.

- INSTRUCTIVE. Even though you may love to do the activities, they are actually training your brain and body to stop overreacting. Doing them is like sending your brain and senses to their own special school, where they learn how to work together better.

- HELPFUL. If you do these activities, you just might be able to enjoy what you want to enjoy, succeed better at anything you try to do, learn more easily at school, be calmer when things start to get upsetting, and think "I can do it!" more than "I can't do it!"

*"You will probably want to do some of these activities for years and years, just because they feel so good."*

## The Five Activity Types

Each activity will always be one of these five types.

1. **A do-it-yourself activity.** This means you do the activity without anyone else helping you. Maybe an adult could check to see how you are doing every now and then.

2. **A partner activity.** You do the activity with another child or an adult. Often the other person is a brother, sister, classmate, friend, parent, therapist, teacher, or OT.

3. **A sitting or lying-down activity.** This is a partner activity in which your role is to sit or lie still while the other person does something that involves one of your sense organs, such as rubbing your skin.

4. **Help for your brain or body.** You give help to your brain, such as eating "brain food." Or you give help to

your body, such as rubbing a soothing lotion onto your skin.

5. **Meeting a need of your senses.** A need is met, such as turning down a light that is too bright or changing into a shirt made from smoother, less scratchy fabric.

## STEP 2: REPORT YOUR RESULTS

What if your OT suggests fun activities for you, and you do them often. Then, after a few weeks, you might notice that loud sounds don't bother you as much, or that clothes or cloth doesn't seem so rough on your skin. Your OT needs to know about your good news! What if you DON'T tell your OT about your good news? Then your OT might think the activities aren't helping you, and might even tell you to stop doing them! It is VERY important that you not only *do* the activities, but that you also *tell* your parent or OT about what happens after you do them.

### Be Like a Scientist

Scientists notice results and write them down, so they can talk about them with other scientists. Scientists also know that results are often little tiny bits of change, not great big changes all at once. So don't expect HUGE changes after just a few times of doing an activity. Be like a scientist and expect SMALL changes over a LONG period of time as you do your activities.

Scientists also know that they must do their experiments exactly right, or the results won't come out right. In the same way, you must do the activities *exactly* as your OT says to do them. What if you do them a different way, and they don't work? Maybe they would have worked if you did it the way the OT said to do it! The only way for you to tell that an activity helps you is to do it *exactly* the way the OT thinks you are doing it.

So, be like a scientist in three ways:

1. Do the "experiment" exactly as your OT wants you to do it.

2. Report the results to your parent or your OT.

3. Expect small changes over a long period of time.

## How to Report Your Results

Whenever you notice anything different about how an activity feels to you, talk about it. Pretend you are a scientist, reporting the results of your experiment to other scientists. You can also have a special meeting, called a "Personal Private Interview" (see chapter 10), about once a month to talk to your parent about any changes you notice from doing the activities.

Not only **do** the activities, but also **tell** your parent or OT about **what** happens after you do them.

Sometimes an OT will want a child to talk to another adult about the results. There could be many helpers who might want to talk to you about the results of your activities. Ask your parent or OT about who else should know about your results. I'm sure there will be lots of people who will be happy to hear your good news!

Here are some types of adults who often help kids stop overreacting to their senses:

*Physical therapist:* A person trained in sensory issues of the muscles and moving body parts, such as arms and legs

*Counselor:* A person trained in helping family members get along better with each other

*Speech and language therapist:* A person trained in sensory issues inside and outside the mouth

*Physician:* A doctor trained in keeping people healthy and curing diseases

*Special teacher:* A teacher trained in different ways of teaching kids with special learning needs

Sometimes there is no OT to help, but one of these other helpers can help you. When this book says "OT," but you are being helped by one of these other helpers, pretend that this book is talking about the one helping you, even though that person may not be an OT.

## Speak Up about Your Senses!

If something bothers you, be sure to let the adults know. They might be able to change things around in your classroom or at home so you aren't bothered so much. Or, they might find an activity that will help you. But if you don't tell them what bothers you, they won't know which activity to suggest for you to do or what changes to make to help you.

If you think you need a break, a rest, or a time-out to calm down, be sure to ask your parent or teacher to help you. If you stay silent and don't speak up about your sensory needs, the adults can't help you as much.

## The Four Big Reasons Kids Say, "I Don't Want To"

Here are the four big reasons why kids who overreact to senses don't want to try the activities. Do any of these describe your feelings about doing them?

1. I'm afraid they'll make me too different from who I am.

2. I'm afraid they'll make me like things I don't want to like.

3. I'm afraid I would do them just to please an adult, not because I want to do them.

4. I'm afraid I would look funny doing them.

Notice that each of these "reasons" is actually a fear. Here are the answers to these four fears.

**FEAR #1:** I'm afraid they'll make me too different from who I am.

**Answer:** The only differences will be that you are bothered less than you are now by what you hear,

*"notice that each of these 'reasons' is actually a fear."*

taste, smell, feel, or see. As a result, you will be better able to do whatever you wish to do!

**FEAR #2:** I'm afraid of no longer controlling my likes and dislikes.

**Answer:** You will still be free to dislike hearing certain sounds or feeling certain cloth against your skin, but it won't bother you as much. The fact that it won't bother you as much doesn't mean you have to like it. You can still choose not to like it.

**FEAR #3:** I'm afraid I would do them just to please an adult, not because I want to do them.

**Answer:** The basic reason for doing the activities is not to make adults happy. It is to make you happy! Only if they love you and care about you will they be happy and pleased that you are doing the activities. Take their joy that you are doing the activities as proof that they love and care about you.

**FEAR #4:** I'm afraid of looking funny to others.

**Answer:** These activities are often done by people who are just having fun. Some are even games people play at parties! Those that involve special equipment can always be done in private anyway, if you wish.

# Now You're Ready to
# TRAIN YOUR BRAIN!

Always remember the three steps we talked about:

**Step 1:** Do your activities every day.

**Step 2:** Report any changes to the adults who are helping you.

**Step 3:** Give your brain what it needs—nutrition, sleep, and protection from stress chemicals and outside chemicals.

Always be aware of what your sensory needs are and of what bothers you when you feel, taste, smell, see, or hear. The best way to stop overreacting is to get plenty of practice at handling sensory messages in a calmer way. The five types of activities will help your brain and body learn to stop overreacting. Let's start with your skin, and the sense of touch!

*"The best way to stop overreacting is to get plenty of practice at handling sensory messages in a calmer way."*

# CHAPTER 3

# Learn to Have Fun with Touch

Your skin is the largest sense organ in your body. It never stops working and is always sending messages to your brain, even when you are asleep!

## DO YOU OVERREACT TO TOUCH?

Here is a quiz about your sense of touch. See how many times you answer YES!

*NO means "I'm bothered sometimes, seldom, or never." YES means "I'm bothered usually or often."*

### AM I BOTHERED BY:

Bathing, showering,
   or drying off with a towel    ☐ YES   ☐ NOT SURE   ☐ NO

Having my hair brushed, combed, cut,
   shampooed, or dried    ☐ YES   ☐ NOT SURE   ☐ NO

Getting drops of water on my
face or cheek    ☐ YES    ☐ NOT SURE    ☐ NO

Tight-fitting collars, stretch bands, cuffs,
turtlenecks, or hats    ☐ YES    ☐ NOT SURE    ☐ NO

Loose-fitting collars
or cuffs    ☐ YES    ☐ NOT SURE    ☐ NO

Tags, seams, or cuffs
on my clothing    ☐ YES    ☐ NOT SURE    ☐ NO

Clothing that is not extremely smooth
(not made of silk, nylon,
or soft cotton)    ☐ YES    ☐ NOT SURE    ☐ NO

Clothing that is extremely smooth
(such as silk)    ☐ YES    ☐ NOT SURE    ☐ NO

Being touched lightly
or as a surprise    ☐ YES    ☐ NOT SURE    ☐ NO

Being hugged or
cuddled    ☐ YES    ☐ NOT SURE    ☐ NO

Very light touch, such as by a feather or being tickled with fingertips    ☐ YES    ☐ NOT SURE    ☐ NO

Deep touch, such as a bear hug
or massage    ☐ YES    ☐ NOT SURE    ☐ NO

Messy textures, such as finger-paints, paste,
mud, toothpaste, or
papier-mâché paste    ☐ YES    ☐ NOT SURE    ☐ NO

Playing in a sandbox or handling
sand or rice    ☐ YES    ☐ NOT SURE    ☐ NO

Having my fingernails
trimmed      ☐ YES    ☐ NOT SURE    ☐ NO

Brushing or flossing my teeth, whether by myself or with
an adult helping me      ☐ YES    ☐ NOT SURE    ☐ NO

How did you rate yourself? If you answered "No" to every item, your brain handles touch messages the same way most kids do. If you answered "Yes" to any item, discuss your answers with your parent or OT to see how he or she can help you.

# TAKE CHARGE

## Plan Ahead for Outdoor Events

When you're going to an outdoor event, such as a ball game, bring along comfortable seating, such as a thick blanket that is easy to brush off, or a folding chair or camp stool. Also be prepared for any weather, so it doesn't bother you so much. If it might rain or snow, for example, bring along a hood or a hat with a brim, a jacket, and an umbrella.

## Avoid Surprises

Being touched by surprise is often a bigger problem than being touched in a way that you know in advance is going to happen. Ask those who are going to touch you to approach you from the front, so you can be ready to receive their touch.

## Healthy Skin Is Less Sensitive

Another way to have fewer problems with touch is to make sure your skin is healthy. For good skin health, drink plenty of water and eat foods with helpful fatty acids and minerals (we'll talk more about this in chapter 8). Tanned skin is unhealthy, so avoid getting a tan. Use mild soaps and shampoo when you wash, and ask your parents to use laundry soaps and detergents that don't have harsh chemicals in them. They will say "hypoallergenic" or "organic" or "all natural" or "additive free" on the label.

## Choose Your Clothes Wisely

When you're shopping for clothes or choosing what to wear, avoid clothes with bands of elastic at the wrist or ankles, sewn-in patterns that could rub against your skin, tight collars, and elastic waistbands. Select tightly fitting clothes if you like pressure on your skin and choose loose-fitting clothes if you don't like pressure on your skin. If the tags inside shirt and blouse collars bother you, ask your parent to cut them off for you. Also, ask your parent about cutting off any loose threads inside the seams of your socks.

If buttons or zippers give you trouble, ask your parent for Velcro and pull-up waistbands. When you get new clothes, wash them in a washing machine before wearing them. Clothes will also feel better on your skin if they have been treated with fabric softener when they were in the washer or dryer.

> "When you get **new clothes, wash** them in a washing machine **before wearing** them."

## When You Can't Avoid It

If you can't avoid being touched in a way that bothers you, there are several things you can do. One is to listen to pleasant music at the time. Feeling "heavy" also makes touch less noticeable. Try wearing a weighted belt or vest that has pockets you can put weights into. Try draping a heavy quilt over yourself or having an adult press down on your head. Another way to learn to tolerate unpleasant touch is to find something to do with your hands, such as holding or gently squeezing a favorite toy or doll.

> "If you **can't avoid** being **touched** in a way that **bothers you**, there are several **things you can do**.

## What to Do during Grooming

If you are bothered by touch when you're having your hair washed, ask your parent to massage your scalp first and to wash your hair with a bath mitt rather than with bare hands. During the hair rinse, hold a washcloth over your face or use a foam visor so you get less shampoo or water on your face. You can use earplugs so nothing gets into your ears. When you're getting your hair brushed, use a tangle-free conditioner and a brush with long bristles that bend. If you can brush your own hair, it might not feel as bad.

If having your hair cut bothers you, put some baby powder on your skin after the haircut. Instead of wearing a tight plastic cape, try a towel clipped loosely behind your neck. Have a shirt or blouse ready to change into, so you don't have tiny hairs poking at you after the haircut! To make teeth-brushing go better, rub your fingers over your gums before you brush your teeth, and be in charge of setting the water temperature. Pour yourself a little cup of water, and wet your toothbrush every few strokes. Try brushing your teeth without toothpaste for most of the time, then use just a little bit of toothpaste with a few brush strokes before rinsing. Try different flavors of toothpaste to find one you really like. Maybe you can choose your own toothbrush, or even try different electric brushes!

If having your nails trimmed bothers you, apply skin lotion to your hands first to help soften them. You can also take a bath or shower first, so they are easier to trim. One good thing about having your nails trimmed is that you can do it lying down. So lie down and listen to some soft music during the trimming. Sometimes having your nails trimmed by a parent when you are asleep works best of all, because you don't even feel anything!

## Slowly Get Used to It

One way to react less to touch is to practice feeling touch that doesn't bother you. Then, slowly try touch that is a little more rough. Find a type of cloth that feels okay, and rub it gently on your skin. Then find a cloth that is a little bit rougher and rub that one on your skin. Keep finding more types of cloth to try, and practice every day. Soon you might find that you can stand many more types of cloth on your skin.

Your parent or OT can help decrease your overreaction to touch by doing the same kind of thing for you while you lie down on a sofa. Stay relaxed as your legs are stroked with items that are a tiny bit different each time. The adult will stop when you say you can't stay relaxed while feeling that item. The exact items and the order in which they are rubbed across your legs should be decided by the adult helping you. For example, she might start by rubbing a soft ball of cotton on your leg, then soft cloth, then fur, then a fluffy towel, then a washcloth. Do this activity every day, so your brain gets lots of practice at learning to accept different kinds of touch messages. This activity is one of the easiest you can ever do—just lie down and stay relaxed. It is also fun to take different textures and rub them on your parent's skin!

Another way that many OTs help kids is by moving special brushes across their skin and gently squeezing them at the shoulders and elbows. Most kids who overreact to touch like the way the brush and the gentle squeezing feel. It is probably NOT a good idea to have a lot of different brushes going across your skin, unless your OT guides you in which brushes to use and how to move them across your skin.

# now You're Ready to TRAIN YOUR BRAIN!

To train your brain to stop overreacting to touch, give it plenty of practice at receiving messages about firm touch from your skin. Firm, predictable, deep-pressure touch is easier to take than light and unexpected touch and will give your brain a chance to experience a wide variety of touch messages. Here are some activities you can try. Select the ones you would like to do, and discuss them with your parent or OT. Your OT might also suggest activities other than those listed here!

## Firm-Touch Activities

### 1. Play "I'm a Sandwich."

You get to be the meat on a sandwich. Lie face down on the bottom "slice of bread" or "bottom bun," which can be a gym mat, cushion, sofa, bed, or folded blanket. An adult can use firm, downward strokes with a "spreader," such as a sponge, vegetable brush, paintbrush, or washcloth to smear your arms, legs, tummy, back, and neck with pretend condiments, such as water or lotion. Then you get covered with the top slice of bread, or "top bun," which can be a clean doormat, throw rug, comforter, shawl, sheet, blanket, or beach towel. If you think you would like how it feels, the adult can even press the top "bun" to squish out the excess condiments!

2. **Play "I'm a Burrito."**

Play this game in the same way as "I'm a Sandwich," but instead of being between two buns, you get rolled up in a blanket as your burrito shell!

3. **Play "Steamroller" with a ball.**

An adult firmly rolls a big ball over your body, arms, and legs while pressing down on the ball.

4. **Play "I'm a Pizza."**

Your parent rolls a ball over you as you say "tomatoes," "mushrooms," "cheese," or whatever you think would be fun to have on you if you were a real pizza.

## Activities for a Variety of Touches

1. **Play "Guess What I'm Drawing."**

An adult draws something on your arm, your back, your tummy, your leg, your palm, the top of your foot, or the back of your hand. You get to guess what was drawn. To make it more fun, the adult owes you a penny every time you are right, and you owe the adult a penny every time you are wrong with your first guess!

### 2. Play "What's Inside the Sack?"

Your parent finds objects at home that are rough, smooth, scratchy, soft, hard, pointed, heavy, and light. She puts them into a grocery sack or pillowcase. You reach in and, without looking, describe each object by the way it feels. After you describe it, bring it out and put it in a small pile. If you want, you can arrange the items by size, shape, weight, or color. When you're done, help put them back where they came from!

### 3. Play "What's Inside the Box?"

An adult gets a shoebox and cuts a hole in the lid, about the size of a baseball. Then she places spools, buttons, blocks, coins, marbles, marshmallows, small toys, and other items inside. You get to put your hand through the hole and, without looking, guess what the objects are. Next, have the adult give you a clue to help you feel around for one special object among all the ones in the box.

### 4. Play "Pirate Treasure."

An adult gathers small pieces of "treasure," such as macaroni, beans, rice, pasta, wet strips of paper, popcorn, (popped and unpopped), marbles, and wet noodles. In a bucket, deep bowl, cooking pot, or sandbox (or at the beach!), the adult buries the treasure in the sand (or you could use cornmeal if you're indoors). With your eyes closed, you find the buried treasure and name each item as you find it. For extra fun, maybe the adult can include a few real coins or a dollar bill among the treasure items!

5. **Stroke a furry pet** while you hold it on your lap for at least 2 minutes.

6. **Play "How Many Times."**

   An adult touches your back with one, two, or three fingertips at the exact same time. You get to guess how many fingers were used, called "touch points." This game is harder than it sounds!

7. **Experiment with liquids and gels.**

   Your parent gently rubs liquids and gels on your skin, such as oatmeal soap, skin lotion, body lotion, shaving cream, whipped cream, or yogurt. A great time to give your brain this kind of practice at feeling liquids is right before you take a bath or shower!

8. **Experiment with rougher items.**

   Your parent can stroke your skin gently with items like a sponge, a thick washcloth, a foam pot-scrubber, an oven mitt, a vegetable brush, a paintbrush, a plastic dish scrubber, or bubble wrap. This way, your brain gets practice at feeling touch that is a tiny bit rough!

9. **Take a "Super Bath!"**

   Fill a portable tub or backyard pool with bubble bath or some soap and water, then put things in it that can safely go underwater, like plastic pitchers, plastic bottles, sponges, egg beaters for making froth, spoons, and plastic cups. You can sit in the water, pour the soapy water in and out of everything, and have lots of sensory fun. Be sure to rinse yourself off with pure water after taking this "super bath."

10. **Play with things you have to push and pull** slightly with your hands, such as finger-paints, play dough, crazy putty, cookie batter, or pizza dough.

11. **Play "Come to My Store."**

    Pretend to buy and sell objects with various textures, such as rice, gelatin, cornmeal, yarn, leather, a chain necklace, and marshmallows, and put each item into a small plastic sandwich bag when you sell it. You can even use plastic play money and put a piece of paper next to each item with its price. Then ask everyone in your family to come to your store!

12. **Have your parent warm up your towel in the clothes dryer,** so you have a warm towel to dry off with after your bath or shower, or just to wrap yourself in for fun. Maybe your parent can even give you a deep, slow massage with the warm towel.

## Activities for Your Feet

1. Wade in a backyard pool.

2. Ask your parent to give you a gentle, dry foot massage, or one using body lotion.

3. Play "Happy Feet."

   While your parent is sitting on a sofa, lie down and put your bare feet on your parent's lap. Your parent can give you a gentle foot rub. Ask your parent to massage each of your toes, one at a time! This is a great activity to do while watching TV or a DVD or listening to music together.

## Activities for Your Mouth

1. Practice various kinds of blowing. You can blow whistles and candles, blow through a straw into a dish of bubbles, or blow cotton balls across a table by blowing through a straw. Or, try blowing feathers on a table, bubbles off of a wand, a kazoo, a harmonica, or even milk through a loopy straw to make bubbles and froth!

2. An adult can give you a bowl of foods that are sort of crunchy, such as celery sticks, carrot sticks, broccoli, sunflower seeds, pumpkin seeds, or mixed nuts. Eat them very slowly, and see if you can taste each item without looking to guess what it is!

3. Suck a thick, yummy fruit smoothie through a straw, or even applesauce through a thick straw.

4. Suck on your favorite juice through a little straw placed in a juice box, cup, or glass.

5. Chew dried fruit or a fruit strip. Good dried fruits to try are cherries, cranberries, bananas, pineapple, apricots, peaches, raisins, and prunes!

## DO IT!

Now you know many ways to have fun with your sense of touch. Choose the activities you would like to try, and discuss them with your parent or OT.

Next we'll move on to another sense that involves the skin—the sense of movement!

# CHAPTER 4

# Learn to Have Fun with Movement

## Did You Know?

Your sense of movement is a key to how all of your other senses work. When you sense movement, you also sense the pull of gravity and how balanced you are. If you're feeling upset, creating small movement, such as slowly rocking back and forth, is a great way to calm down. Working your large muscles is also calming, like playing tug-of-war or a push-pull game, taking wet clothes from the washer and putting them into the dryer, or pulling the garden hose around as you water plants.

## DO YOU OVERREACT TO MOVEMENT?

Here is a quiz about your sense of movement. See how many times you answer YES!

*NO means "I'm bothered sometimes, seldom, or never." YES means "I'm bothered usually or often."*

## AM I BOTHERED WHEN I:

Use a playground apparatus, such as a slide, swing, or teeter-totter ☐ YES ☐ NOT SURE ☐ NO

Use an elevator or escalator ☐ YES ☐ NOT SURE ☐ NO

Move fast in one direction, such as riding, sliding, or running ☐ YES ☐ NOT SURE ☐ NO

Move in a circle, such as on a whirling apparatus at the playground, or when I twirl, play circle games, watch others move in circles, square dance, or get spun around ☐ YES ☐ NOT SURE ☐ NO

Ride a large carnival ride, like a carousel, giant swing, or Ferris wheel ☐ YES ☐ NOT SURE ☐ NO

Am moved by another person while I stay in the same body position ☐ YES ☐ NOT SURE ☐ NO

Ride a tire swing while it's pushed in circles ☐ YES ☐ NOT SURE ☐ NO

Am high up or on a raised area, like a platform, ramp, stadium seat, or hilltop ☐ YES ☐ NOT SURE ☐ NO

Am in a chair when it is being moved slightly ☐ YES ☐ NOT SURE ☐ NO

Go up or down stairs ☐ YES ☐ NOT SURE ☐ NO

Have my head tilted or moved far forward or back ☐ YES ☐ NOT SURE ☐ NO

Tilt my head up, such as to catch a baseball or fly a kite ☐ YES ☐ NOT SURE ☐ NO

| | | | |
|---|---|---|---|
| Ride a bicycle | ☐ YES | ☐ NOT SURE | ☐ NO |
| Do anything where my feet leave the ground | ☐ YES | ☐ NOT SURE | ☐ NO |
| Am rocked, such as in a rocking chair | ☐ YES | ☐ NOT SURE | ☐ NO |
| Am picked up and lifted high | ☐ YES | ☐ NOT SURE | ☐ NO |
| Am pushed or pulled in a wagon | ☐ YES | ☐ NOT SURE | ☐ NO |
| Step up to sit on a high stool | ☐ YES | ☐ NOT SURE | ☐ NO |
| Ride in a car, van, bus, or truck | ☐ YES | ☐ NOT SURE | ☐ NO |
| Jump on anything like a mattress, a miniature trampoline, or a large trampoline | ☐ YES | ☐ NOT SURE | ☐ NO |
| Make active movements, such as moving like an animal, doing jumping jacks, dancing, twirling, and jumping rope | ☐ YES | ☐ NOT SURE | ☐ NO |
| Have my head upside down, like with somersaults, tumbling, gymnastics, or handstands | ☐ YES | ☐ NOT SURE | ☐ NO |
| Hold or squeeze anything like a rubber ball, tennis ball, or sponge | ☐ YES | ☐ NOT SURE | ☐ NO |

How did you rate yourself? If you answered "No" to every item, your brain handles movement messages the same way most kids do. If you answered "Yes" to any item, discuss your answers with your parent or OT to see how he or she can help you.

# TAKE CHARGE

If you are bothered by movement, you will feel better if your chair doesn't wobble and if you feel "heavy," such as by wearing a weighted vest or fishing weights tied to your belt. Or, drape a quilt over yourself as you sit. Your OT might show you some fun movement activities called "Brain Gym," which are very popular with kids who are bothered by movement. You can do them in a couple of minutes and just about anywhere.

One of the nice things about going for a walk with a friend or your parent is that you can control your speed and the size of the steps you take. Walking can be a really fun thing to do. Another kind of activity your OT might invite you to do is ride a slow-moving horse. You don't hold the reins—you just sit in the saddle and ride! The horse is driven by an adult who sits behind you or walks next to you. Sometimes sitting backwards in the saddle is easier, because the world is moving away from you instead of coming at you!

## now You're Ready to TRAIN YOUR BRAIN!

To train your brain to stop overreacting to movement, give it plenty of practice at receiving messages from sense organs in your inner ear and muscles.

Give your brain chances to experience different types of movement, like ones that are:

- Using big muscles
- Slow
- Slight
- Up and down
- Pressing
- Near the ground
- Back and forth

Here are some activities you can try. Select the ones you would like to do and discuss them with your parent or OT. They might also suggest activities other than those listed here!

## Activities That Use Big Muscles

1. **Enjoy a friendly, safe pillow fight** by using very soft foam pillows.

2. **Tow a friend in a wagon or sled.**

3. **Walk like an animal,** such as a bear or crab, or do frog jumps, bunny hops, or mule kicks.

4. Have a friend pick up your feet, and **do a "wheelbarrow walk"** on your hands.

5. **Dance with your palms pressed firmly against your partner's palms,** either with or without music!

6. **Play "Acrobat."**

   You are an acrobat, who performs jumping stunts on a rebounder (a mini-trampoline). Your partner assigns you the stunts, like "jump three times on your right foot, then once on your left foot."

**7. Play "Jumping Beans."**

Your partner marks shapes on the floor with masking tape, and you jump in and out of the shapes. Your partner gives you commands, like jumping backward or sideways or hopping on one foot.

**8. Move to music, alone or with a partner.** For example, you could march with your knees up high or walk on your tiptoes!

**9. Play "Design Dance."**

You and your partner make designs with lengths of rope laid out on the floor to form giant letters, numbers, or designs. Then walk or "dance" through the designs, without stepping on any of the rope!

**10. Play "Invent My Dance."**

While music plays, you create movements, like bend, twist, stretch, turn, march, hop, jump, and shake. You control the amount and speed of the movement. Use as many body parts as possible!

**11. Play "Magic Path."**

Your partner sets out paper plates on a lawn or on the floor of a big room. You step only on the plates as you go down your Magic Path. For more fun, mark some of the plates with markers, crayons, or paint, and make those the only ones you can walk on. You aren't allowed to step on the other ones!

12. **Play "Follow the Pop Road."**

Pop some "poppers" (fireworks) placed in a giant pattern on a sidewalk, playground, or driveway.

13. **Play "Double Jumper."**

An adult can put a plastic wading pool (the kind that you pump up) in the center of a full-sized trampoline. Then you get to jump in your own space, and stay safe inside the wading pool!

14. **Play "Mini-Basketball."**

Throw soft objects into a large box or target. You can try wads of paper or ping-pong balls. Lay a piece of rope or string on the floor as your "foul line" to stand behind when you throw.

15. **Hang by your arms** on a chin-up bar or a monkey bar, and shift your grip from hand to hand.

## Pressing Activities

1. **Play "Back to Back."**

Sit with your partner on the floor, back to back. Keep your feet on the floor and stand up together by pressing against each other's backs!

2. **Play "Handy Hands."**

Have an adult sew two oven mitts together at the thumbs. Then, you can wear the oven mitts and wash the walls, countertops, refrigerator door and sides, and appliance doors. Or, you can wipe the chalkboard or white board, desks, play surfaces, or car!

2. **Arm wrestle.**

3. **Dig holes and plant flowers in them. Get rid of weeds by digging them out.**

4. **Play tug of war.**

5. **Push a stroller, vacuum, or similar object across a large room.**

6. **Rake some leaves or garden soil.**

7. **Play "Huggy Bear."**

Give your parent bear hugs. Make a game of how often you hug and when, each day. You can even assign a special word as the "Huggy Bear" word, and every time your parent says that word, you say "Huggy Bear!" And your parent has to give you a hug.

## Activities with Slow Movements

1. **Play "Cleared for Landing."**

Pretend you are an airplane, coming in for a landing. Your parent can pick you up and twirl you slowly, tell you that you are "cleared for landing," then gently place you on a couch, a pile of pillows, or a bed.

2. **Slide slowly down a playground slide** in various positions, with an adult walking next to you all the way down.

3. **Play "Body Rocker."**

   Press your hands against a firm surface, such as a wall, then extend and bend your arms so that your body rocks back and forth slightly toward and slightly away from the wall.

4. **Cross your arms, and press down** on your shoulders with your hands.

5. **Slowly rub your hands along your arms.**

6. **Walk with jingling holiday bells** strapped to your shoes or ankles.

7. **Carefully step onto the cracks as you walk along a sidewalk.** Or, do the opposite, making sure to avoid stepping directly onto any cracks.

8. **Play hopscotch or similar games.**

## Activities Done On or Near the Ground

1. **Roll down a safe, grassy hill.**

2. **Roll around on a large ball.**

3. **Roll across the floor.**

4. **Play "Move the Statue."**

   Pretend you are a statue. Sit or lie in various positions while two adults drag you across the floor in a blanket or sheet. Stay in your position, even if you start to fall over inside the blanket or sheet!

5. **Play "Story Moves."**

   As you take a walk with a friend, make up a story. Go through motions of the story while you walk along. For even more fun, take turns making up each next sentence of the story!

6. **Play "Rock-a-Bye Baby."**

   Lie with your tummy down and your head up on the floor. Try rocking from side to side, drawing on paper with crayons, or playing with small toys.

7. **Lie with your tummy down and your head up on a large ball (called a "therapy ball").** Your OT will probably have one for you to use. While you're draped over the ball, draw on the carpet with a stick, or throw sponges or wads of paper into a basket!

8. Have an adult help you hang a ball from a string. Then, **bat at the ball by using a long cardboard tube or a plastic bat.**

9. **Play "Piano Ride."**

   For this game, you'll need to have an adult make a dolly. She can use a throw rug to cover a flat board mounted on four wheels. Then, you get to ride it! Sit and lie in various ways. The dolly can be pulled by a rope, or you can use your hands or legs to move it. This is a great way to calm down when you need it. You can lie on your side, your back, or your tummy as an adult slowly moves the dolly back and forth.

## Activities with Slight Movements

1. **Sip from a water bottle.**

2. **Do finger exercises.**

3. **Rock gently on a seat cushion** that you blow up with air.

4. **Reach up and down,** going higher and lower as you go.

5. **Press your palms together.**

6. **Pull on each finger of each hand, in order.**

7. **Squeeze a ball or a balloon** filled with sand, rice, or salt.

8. **Play "Giant Octopus."**

   An adult can cut eight thick rubber bands with scissors, then tie them together in the middle with strong fishing line. Now you have a giant octopus with 16 legs, not just eight! You can hold it in your hand, squeeze it, and play with it however you want.

9. **Make things out of modeling clay or play dough.**

10. **Use a pencil as a mini-baton** by twirling it and passing it through your fingers.

11. **Sit on a stool with a seat that turns,** so you can make small turns to the left and right when you sit on it.

12. **Another stool that allows small movement is called a T-stool.** Ask your OT about letting you sit on one!

13. **Bounce on a therapy ball, beach ball, inner tube, or pogo stick.**

14. **Play catch** with water-filled balloons, weighted balls, beanbags, beach balls, therapy balls, boiled eggs, or potatoes.

15. **Bend, then unbend your fingers, wrists, elbows, knees, ankles, or toes.** This activity is great when you are in a small space, such as a church pew, the back seat of a car, an elevator, a theater, a bus, or a plane.

16. When you're sitting in a chair, **shift from side to side.**

17. **Move your shoulders from side to side.**

18. **Pour sand, water, beans, cornmeal, or rice back and forth** from one container to another.

19. **Peel tangerines or oranges with your bare hands.** Do it over a bowl so the peelings go into the bowl. Then enjoy eating the fruit you peeled!

20. **String beads and count them as you string them.** You can string them in a pattern or a special order, such as red-yellow-green or big-medium-little.

21. **Turn over flat objects** like checkers, poker chips, or Tiddlywinks chips with your fingertips, without using the edge of the table to help you. To make it even more challenging, give yourself a time limit!

22. **Sort, stack, make designs with, and count** coins, checkers, or poker chips.

23. Play "Secretary."

Put sheets of paper together with various types and sizes of paper clips and binder clips. Then count the sheets of paper in each clipped bundle!

24. **Sort, stack, and count small objects** like beans or beads, and keep them separated by putting them into the sections of an egg carton.

25. While you're writing or coloring, **hold cotton balls in the same hand you are using to write or color.**

26. Play **"Giant Grabber."**

Gather a bunch of small toys that are tiny versions of huge things, such as cars, buses, trucks, motorcycles, houses, or airplanes. Put them in a row. Then become the "giant grabber" by using kitchen or barbecue tongs to grip the objects and move them from one container to another or one location to another. Pretend your tongs are giant machines lifting real cars, buses, or houses!

27. **With your eyes closed, write letters and numbers on a chalkboard.**

28. **Erase a chalkboard or white board, then wash it with a sponge.**

29. Play **"Super Drawing."**

Fill a large, flat pan with cornmeal, rice, shaving cream, sand, whipped cream from a can, or cornstarch. Then, take your finger and make designs, letters, and numbers!

30. **Play "Mini-Ball Race."**

Make a figure eight on a pizza pan with colored tape. Then, roll a ping-pong ball or a golf ball along the tape. You can change the pattern, and for an added challenge, make a time limit! This activity is great for having a contest, such as during a party.

31. **Play rhyming games with hand movements,** like "Itsy-Bitsy Spider" and "Thumbkin."

## Activities with Back-and-Forth Movements

1. **Play "Two-Minute Hammock."**

   Have two adults swing you back and forth in a blanket or sheet for 2 minutes. You can change your position every so often, and even listen to music while you swing!

2. **Swing back and forth** on a tire swing or a playground swing.

3. **Rock back and forth** in a rocking chair or a porch swing.

## Activities with Up-and-Down Movements

1. **Jump on a pogo stick.**

2. **Hop on a "hoppity hop" type of giant ball** (with a handle to hold on to).

3. **Ride a tire swing** hanging by many strong bungee cords.

# DO IT!

Now you know many great ways to have fun with your sense of movement. Choose the activities you would like to try and discuss them with your parent or OT.

Next, let's talk about your sense of hearing!

# CHAPTER 5

# Learn to Have Fun with Your Hearing

## Did You Know?

You can hear with one ear, but to figure out exactly where a sound is coming from, you need both ears. When you overreact to this sense, you might cover your ears or feel afraid when you hear loud noises.

## DO YOU OVERREACT TO SOUND?

Here is a quiz about your sense of hearing. See how many times you answer YES!

*NO means "I'm bothered sometimes, seldom, or never." YES means "I'm bothered usually or often."*

### AM I BOTHERED BY:

Loud sounds, such as a car horn, a fire alarm, a siren, loud music, a jet plane, or a train whistle

☐ YES ☐ NOT SURE ☐ NO

Very high-pitched sounds, such as a
   wind chime, a bell, a referee's whistle, a violin,
   or a lady singing      ☐ YES   ☐ NOT SURE   ☐ NO

A noise or a voice that I didn't expect or
   that surprises me      ☐ YES   ☐ NOT SURE   ☐ NO

Appliance noise, like a dishwasher, sewing
   machine, dryer, washing machine,
   or vacuum cleaner      ☐ YES   ☐ NOT SURE   ☐ NO

A noise or a voice that I'm not
   used to hearing      ☐ YES   ☐ NOT SURE   ☐ NO

Having to hear the noise from a crowd or the noises
   made at places like a rodeo, a race, a parade,
   a carnival, a stadium, a school assembly,
   a party, a busy store, a restaurant,
   or a large audience   ☐ YES   ☐ NOT SURE   ☐ NO

Being in a group or a room with busy people who
   are talking a lot      ☐ YES   ☐ NOT SURE   ☐ NO

Loud booms, such as thunder, balloons popping,
   fireworks, or gunshots☐ YES   ☐ NOT SURE   ☐ NO

Metallic sounds, such as cymbals, silverware,
   wind chimes, or keys   ☐ YES   ☐ NOT SURE   ☐ NO

Sounds that don't bother other people, like a toilet
   flushing, a far-away church bell ringing,
   or a cell phone      ☐ YES   ☐ NOT SURE   ☐ NO

Music, the radio, or the TV when the volume is
   not set very low      ☐ YES   ☐ NOT SURE   ☐ NO


How did you rate yourself? If you answered "No" to
every item, your brain handles sounds the same way

most kids do. If you answered "Yes" to any item, discuss your answers with your parent or OT to see how he or she can help you!

"Sit as far away as you can from sources of bothersome noise."

## TAKE CHARGE

If you are bothered by sounds at home or at school, ask for earplugs, earmuffs, or headphones that block out sounds. Sit as far away as you can from sources of bothersome noise. If the sound of water running into the bathtub bothers you, ask your parent to fill the tub before you go into the bathroom to take your bath.

Try to arrange for other sounds around you that will "hide" the sounds that bother you. These other good sounds are sometimes called "white noise." White noise can be made with a white-noise machine, an aquarium with an air pump, an air filter, a fan, or an air conditioner.

"Help your brain experience sounds that are natural, musical, or fun."

When you're away from home, try to avoid noisy places, such as places where steam shovels are digging or where jackhammers are working, train depots, and coffee shops with those noisy coffee machines. Maybe you can duck into a store if a vehicle with a siren comes toward you, like a fire truck or an ambulance. You can also pull a headband over your ears to reduce the noise level.

# Now You're Ready to
# TRAIN YOUR BRAIN!

To train your brain to stop overreacting to sounds, give it lots of practice at receiving messages from your ears. Help it experience sounds that are natural, musical, or fun. Here are some activities you can try. Select the ones you would like to do and discuss them with your parent or OT. Your OT might also suggest activities other than those listed here!

## Natural Sounds

1. **Listen to the sounds in nature**, such as the sounds at the beach, the sound of rain, or the sound the wind makes when it blows.

2. **Listen to CDs of nature sounds** (either with or without music).

3. **Make a recording** the next time there's a thunderstorm or a heavy rain.

4. **Play "Chirp and Chatter."**

   It can be fun to listen to bird language. Set out a bird feeder filled with seed and listen to the sounds the birds make when they come to eat. Soon you will be able to tell when they are calling each other, when a young bird asks its parent to feed it some of the seed, and even when the birds fight each other over the seed. See if you can predict what kind of sound a certain bird will make, before it chirps or chatters!

## Musical Sounds

1. **Listen to various types of music** to find out what kinds you don't mind listening to.

2. **Take lessons** to learn how to play a musical instrument.

3. When you're listening to the radio or a CD, **control the volume** so the sound level is okay with you.

4. **Listen to "low, slow, and no" music**, with low volume, slow beat, and no drum. This is the best kind to listen to in your bedroom to help you get to sleep at night.

5. **Listen to a few minutes of music** with headphones on, at the same time each day.

6. **Listen to music at a very, very low volume**, then slowly increase the volume each minute. Stop turning up the volume when your parent tells you it is about as loud as most people would like it to be. If you do this every day, you might learn to tolerate music playing at a louder volume.

## Sounds as Play

**1. Play "What's That Sound?"**

An adult records various sounds and plays them for you. You guess what each sound is. To make it harder, make sure you don't know where the adult was when the recordings were made, so you don't have any clues!

**2. Play "Sound Around."**

With one or more partners, take turns making a sound and adding it to all the sounds made before it. First you make a sound, then your partner makes that sound, plus a second sound. Then the third person makes both of those sounds, plus a third sound. Keep going until someone can't remember all the sounds in the correct order. Then that person becomes the starter for the next group of sounds.

# DO IT!

We've talked about many ways to have fun with your sense of hearing. Choose the activities you would like to try and discuss them with your parent or OT.

Some kids overreact to what they hear, and some overreact to what they see. The next chapter is about the sense that you use more than any other when you are in school—your vision!

# CHAPTER 6

# Learn to Have Fun with Your Vision

## Did You Know?

At school, you use your vision to do most of your learning. Much of the activity your brain does when your eyes are open has to do with vision. Some children have problems with their vision, and they are bothered by accidentally looking at things they don't want to look at. It is hard for them to keep looking at what they are supposed to be looking at. When this happens, they are "distracted."

## DO YOU OVERREACT TO SIGHT?

Here is a quiz about visual distraction. See how many times you answer YES!

*NO means "I'm bothered or distracted sometimes, seldom, or never." YES means "I'm bothered or distracted usually or often."*

## WHEN I'M READING OR DOING A VISUAL TASK, AM I BOTHERED OR DISTRACTED BY:

Very black and very white colors
on the same page    ☐ YES    ☐ NOT SURE    ☐ NO

Bright lights while I'm
trying to read    ☐ YES    ☐ NOT SURE    ☐ NO

Fluorescent lights while
I'm trying to read    ☐ YES    ☐ NOT SURE    ☐ NO

Sunlight reflecting off shiny areas,
like my desk    ☐ YES    ☐ NOT SURE    ☐ NO

Having to read off of bright
white paper    ☐ YES    ☐ NOT SURE    ☐ NO

Flickering lights    ☐ YES    ☐ NOT SURE    ☐ NO

Moving objects nearby    ☐ YES    ☐ NOT SURE    ☐ NO

Dangling mobiles    ☐ YES    ☐ NOT SURE    ☐ NO

How did you rate yourself? If you answered "No" to every item, it means your brain prevents you from being distracted. If you answered "Yes" to any item, show this quiz to your parent or OT, because you might benefit from some special help.

## Another Fun Quiz for You

Here is a quiz about what happens when you use your vision at school or at home, such as when you're reading or writing at a desk. See how many you answer YES!

*NO means "I hardly ever do this or I never do this." YES means "I do this sometimes or often."*

## WHEN I TRY TO READ, DO I:

Get headaches       ☐ YES    ☐ NOT SURE    ☐ NO

Squint my eyes       ☐ YES    ☐ NOT SURE    ☐ NO

Close or cover one eye    ☐ YES    ☐ NOT SURE    ☐ NO

Rub my eye       ☐ YES    ☐ NOT SURE    ☐ NO

Need a guide, such as
a finger or a ruler    ☐ YES    ☐ NOT SURE    ☐ NO

Hold the paper less than
7 inches from my eyes    ☐ YES    ☐ NOT SURE    ☐ NO

Tilt my head down within
7 inches from the desk    ☐ YES    ☐ NOT SURE    ☐ NO

Lose my place       ☐ YES    ☐ NOT SURE    ☐ NO

Put my hand on my forehead because
the light is too bright    ☐ YES    ☐ NOT SURE    ☐ NO

See the letters "disappear,"
then come back    ☐ YES    ☐ NOT SURE    ☐ NO

See the letters or words
"move" on the page    ☐ YES    ☐ NOT SURE    ☐ NO

See the letters "shake"
or "jiggle"    ☐ YES    ☐ NOT SURE    ☐ NO

See the letters "spin"    ☐ YES    ☐ NOT SURE    ☐ NO

See the letters "break apart"    ☐ YES    ☐ NOT SURE    ☐ NO

See the letters get fuzzy
or blurry    ☐ YES    ☐ NOT SURE    ☐ NO

Get sick to my stomach    ☐ YES    ☐ NOT SURE    ☐ NO

Get dizzy       ☐ YES    ☐ NOT SURE    ☐ NO

Feel burning and itching
   in my eyes        ☐ YES    ☐ NOT SURE    ☐ NO

Get tears in my eyes    ☐ YES    ☐ NOT SURE    ☐ NO

Blink my eyes          ☐ YES    ☐ NOT SURE    ☐ NO

See two letters rather than one letter, for every
   letter on the page    ☐ YES    ☐ NOT SURE    ☐ NO

Stammer and
   reread words       ☐ YES    ☐ NOT SURE    ☐ NO

Accidentally skip numbers, letters,
   words, or lines      ☐ YES    ☐ NOT SURE    ☐ NO

Mix two words together, as if they are one word
   (such as reading the words "into it" as if they are
   one word—"intoit")    ☐ YES    ☐ NOT SURE    ☐ NO

Split words apart (read a six-letter word as if it is
   actually two three-letter words, such as
   reading the word "better" as if it is two words,
   "bet" and "ter")     ☐ YES    ☐ NOT SURE    ☐ NO

Jump lines as you move across the page
   (such as starting on line 6, and winding up
   on line 7)         ☐ YES    ☐ NOT SURE    ☐ NO

How did you rate yourself? If you answered "No" to
every item, it means your brain handles visual messages the same way most kids do. If you answered
"Yes" to any item, show this quiz to your parent or
OT, because you might benefit from some special
help with your eyes.

# TAKE CHARGE

Guard against bright sunlight by wearing a baseball cap, a wide-brimmed bonnet or hat, a sombrero, a sun visor, or a pair of sunglasses. Or, you can hold a parasol or small umbrella to help block out the light. When you're reading, adjust the brightness of the light to a level that's comfortable. Try using pastel-colored paper for reading and writing if bright white paper bothers you. Fluorescent lights can be hard to read under if you are bothered by bright light, so use a regular light bulb in a desk lamp or a floor lamp instead.

*"When you're reading, adjust the brightness of the light to a level that's comfortable."*

A person who could help you if you answered "Yes" to any of the items on the second quiz (about reading) is a *developmental optometrist*. This person has been trained in methods to improve control over eye muscles and might give you special help, called "vision therapy." Your OT can advise you about whether vision therapy would be a good idea.

# TAKE CHARGE AT SCHOOL

There are many visual distractions in most classrooms. Try to sit away from and not look at animal cages, bright displays, flashing lights, dangling mobiles, fluorescent lights, open shelves filled with colorful items, displays fluttering from fans or breezes, doors opening and closing, and multicolor displays. If glare is a problem, wear a visor or baseball cap, ask for a desk away from direct sunlight and glaring lights, and adjust window blinds so sunlight doesn't flicker into your eyes. Also think about asking for a floor lamp with a regular light bulb and a shade to become the main source of lighting at your desk.

To help stay focused when you're sitting at your desk, place a colored place mat underneath your work for visual contrast, tape a posterboard desk border onto your desk, and be sure to clear your desk between tasks. You can make a cardboard picture frame and hold it over whatever you are trying to read at your desk. Also, you can fold a large sheet of paper with math problems on it in half, so you see only half of the page at any one time.

To avoid looking to the side when you are at your desk, make a cardboard wall about 14 inches high and tape it to the edge of your desk so that it dangles down when you don't need it. You can make two or three of them for two or three sides of your desk, and put Velcro on the edges so they will stand up by themselves! Maybe your teacher can arrange to have a special study booth or "special office" for you,  made from a large cardboard box with a desk inside, so you could study there every so often.

# Now You're Ready to
# TRAIN YOUR BRAIN!

To train your brain to stop overreacting to sight, give it plenty of practice at *(1) visual tracking* (following something with your eyes as it moves), *(2) visual identifying* (figuring out what something is by looking at it), and *(3) visual focusing* (keeping your eyes on something for a long time). Here are some activities you can try. Select the ones you would like to do and discuss them with your parent or OT. Your OT might also suggest activities other than the ones listed here!

## Activities for Visual Tracking

**1. Play "Two-Minute Flashlight Tag."**

In a dark room, you and your partner shine two flashlights around the walls, ceiling, and floor. See how many times you can "catch" your partner's light. If you have a timer, you can even make each tag period exactly 2 minutes long. Take turns being the one chased and the one doing the chasing!

**2. Play slow-motion catch with balloons or scarves.**

Juggle with scarves. Juggling is great fun, and you can do it just about anywhere!

3. **Trace pictures from a tracing book.** A tracing book is like a coloring book, but you draw on thin paper you can see through, so you can trace over the picture underneath.

4. **Play "Amazing Mazes."**

An adult draws a maze on paper or on a sidewalk with chalk or sand. You follow the maze with your finger if it's on paper, and with chalk if it's on a sidewalk!

5. **Play "Dot-to-Dot."**

On graph paper, an adult makes dot-to-dot patterns for you to copy on your own sheet of graph paper. Connect the dots when you're done, and color the design to make it into a pretty picture!

6. **Play "Sky Watcher."**

Lie on your back outside and watch for birds, clouds, and planes. Keep your head still, moving only your eyes. For even more fun, put small pieces of bread out to attract more birds!

## Activities for Visual Identifying

1. **Play "See and Spell."**

Your partner gathers a lot of things, the names of which begin with letters that are next to each other in the alphabet, like an **a**pple, a **b**oat, **C**heerios, a **d**uck toy, an **e**gg, and a **f**eather. She keeps them hidden so you can't see them. Then you look at each item and name it. After you name each object, try to put it in alphabetic order with the others. For more fun, give each item a silly name that starts with the same first letter, such as "Barney Banana," "Corny Cork," or "Donkey Dime."

## 2. Play "I Spy."

Pick out an object that you and your partner can both see from where you are. Give your partner a tiny clue, such as "I spy something green." Your partner has to guess what it is. Take turns being the spy and the guesser!

## 3. Play "Build the Alphabet."

When riding as a passenger in a car or truck with other passengers, work together to spot each letter of the alphabet in correct order (everybody except the driver, that is). Look for letters on billboards, road signs, words on trucks, business signs, and license plates. Find an "a," then a "b," then a "c," and so forth. For more fun, give yourselves a distance limit of 5 or 10 miles in which to find all 26 letters.

## Activities for Visual Focusing

## 1. Push dry spaghetti through a straw.

## 2. String some beads.

## 3. Play "Pick-Up Sticks."

In this game, you drop a handful of long, straight sticks onto a table or the floor. Then, you have to try to pick up only one stick at a time without moving or touching the others! You can buy a tube of colored sticks or use ones that are all the same color. You could even play this game with a handful of straws!

**4. Play "Cut and Collect."**

An adult draws shapes or pictures on paper and gives you a pair of scissors to cut out the drawings with. Collect the drawings and make tree ornaments or other decorations from them, or use them to make greeting-card designs!

**5. Recycle old greeting cards** by cutting the pictures out of them and pasting them onto new cards you make.

**6. Make a collage.**

A collage is a piece of paper that has a bunch of pictures and words on it. Make your own by getting some old magazines, glue, scissors, and art paper. Be sure your scissors are the safe kind for kids. Use letters that you cut out of the magazines to build the words for your collage, and add pictures. This is a great activity to do with friends or as a family, with a theme such as "My favorite pet" or "What I did this summer." You can have an art show after everyone is done!

**7. Put together jigsaw puzzles.**

**8. Build small items** with construction toys.

**9. Play "3-D Shapes."**

Draw or make letters, numbers, or designs by using materials such as play dough, finger-paint, shaving cream, soap foam, sand, clay, string, pudding, or pizza dough.

10. **Play "Jewelry Store."**

   A doll or teddy bear could be a customer in your jewelry store. Put play jewelry on the customer, then take it off and put it back into the jewelry box. If you want to use real jewelry, be sure your parent says it's okay first!

# DO IT!

Now you've learned many ways to have fun with your sense of vision. Choose the activities you would like to try and discuss them with your parent or OT.

Other senses are important, too, and the next chapter discusses two of them!

# CHAPTER 7

# Learn to Have Fun with Tastes and Smells

## ——— Did You Know? ———

The senses of taste and smell are connected to each other. Much of what we taste actually comes from what we also smell at the same time. If you're very bothered by the taste of foods, you might find yourself sniffing your food before tasting it or pinching your nose closed while chewing it, because the way it smells has a LOT to do with the way it tastes!

# DO YOU OVERREACT TO TASTE OR SMELL?

Here is a quiz about the senses of taste and smell. See how many times you answer YES!

*NO means "I'm bothered sometimes, seldom, or never." YES means "I'm bothered usually or often."*

## AM I BOTHERED BY:

Foods most children
my age enjoy ☐ YES ☐ NOT SURE ☐ NO

Most foods, so I like only
a few foods ☐ YES ☐ NOT SURE ☐ NO

Tastes that most other kids
aren't bothered by ☐ YES ☐ NOT SURE ☐ NO

Smells that most other kids
aren't bothered by ☐ YES ☐ NOT SURE ☐ NO

Smells that others don't even
know are there ☐ YES ☐ NOT SURE ☐ NO

Strong odors, like perfumes and
cleaning products ☐ YES ☐ NOT SURE ☐ NO

A certain food because
it's too hot ☐ YES ☐ NOT SURE ☐ NO

A certain food because
it's too cold ☐ YES ☐ NOT SURE ☐ NO

A certain food because
it's not hot enough ☐ YES ☐ NOT SURE ☐ NO

A certain food because it's
not cold enough ☐ YES ☐ NOT SURE ☐ NO

A certain food because
   it's too crunchy                □ YES   □ NOT SURE   □ NO

A certain food because
   it's too creamy                 □ YES   □ NOT SURE   □ NO

A certain food because
   it's too grainy                 □ YES   □ NOT SURE   □ NO

A certain food because
   it's too sticky                 □ YES   □ NOT SURE   □ NO

A certain food because
   I've never had it before        □ YES   □ NOT SURE   □ NO

A certain food because it has a strong flavor
   (like spicy, bitter, sour,
   salty, or peppery)              □ YES   □ NOT SURE   □ NO


How did you rate yourself? If you answered "No" to every item, it means your brain handles taste and smell messages the same way most kids do. If you answered "Yes" to any item, discuss your answers with your parent or OT to see how he or she can help you.

## TAKE CHARGE

To be a healthy and happy person, you need to have a lot of different foods to choose from. So learning to like a wide variety of foods is important. One way to make eating more fun is to get involved in all the activities connected to it. Ask your parent to let you help plan the menu at home, do the grocery shopping, select the foods you want to try, and prepare the meals.

"*Learning to like a wide variety of foods is important.*"

When you're helping to prepare the dishes, you should taste them before you serve them. Tasting the food before you serve it tells you how to adjust the recipe for next time. For instance, maybe it tasted a little too salty, so you'll know to add a little less salt the next time. If you're going to be away from home, you can bring along your own food and water so you know you'll have something good to eat.

To avoid strong smells at home, ask your parent to buy all-natural soaps and cleaning supplies. Certain houseplants are great for cleaning the air and getting rid of odors—maybe you can have one in your room. Some of the best plants are a Boston fern, a spider plant, a peace lily, a dwarf date palm, a bamboo palm, a Kimberly Queen fern, a rubber plant, and a florist's mum. Also, you can open a window to get some fresh air! There are also air-filtering machines that you can plug into the wall.

At school, some sources of strong odors are paint, glue, white-board markers, and the soaps the janitor cleans the floors and windows with. White-board markers that don't have an odor are easy for your teacher to get. If odors bother you, try to sit far away from any sources of odors. Maybe your parent can arrange with your teacher to have a window open nearby for fresh air, or the teacher can turn on an electric air-purifying machine. Perhaps your teacher can arrange to have one of those plants that get rid of odors in your classroom!

> "White-board markers that don't have an odor are easy for your teacher to get."

# Now You're Ready to
# TRAIN YOUR BRAIN!

To train your brain to stop overreacting to taste and smell, give it plenty of practice at receiving messages about taste and smell (from your mouth and nose) that are fun and pleasant. Here are some activities you can try. Discuss these with your parent or OT, who might also suggest activities other than the ones listed here.

## Fun and Pleasant Tastes and Smells

**1. Play "What Am I Tasting?"**

Your parent chooses a food for you to taste with your eyes closed. Then you try to figure out what it is by tasting it! For added fun, use a blindfold.

**2. Play "What Am I Smelling?"**

Your parent chooses a pleasant scent for you to smell with your eyes closed. Then you try to figure out what the scent is! You can use a blindfold for this game, too.

3. When you're eating a meal, **eat slowly and think about the various pleasant tastes of the food.** One way to be more aware of what you are eating is to not watch television while you eat.

4. **Use snack time to try new tastes**, such as crunchy, creamy, sweet, salty, chewy, spicy, sour, or lumpy. Start with one bite. If you decide you like the food, you can always take more!

5. **Try sniffing pleasant scents**, such as lavender, rose, vanilla, peppermint, and lemon.

6. **Find various pleasant-scented products to smell**, such as soap, bath oil, baby powder, shampoo, and skin lotion.

# DO IT!

We've talked about lots of ways to have fun with your senses of smell and taste. Choose the activities you would like to try and discuss them with your parent or OT.

The senses of taste and smell help you enjoy eating, and that is what the next chapter is about!

# CHAPTER 8

# Eat the Right Foods

*Eating the right foods* means giving your brain the parts of food that it needs. The good-for-you part of a food is called a "nutrient." If a food has lots of good nutrients in it, it is called "nutritious." Five nutrients that can help your brain do a better job of handling messages from your senses are:

- Amino acids (pronounced uh-MEEN-oh)

- Vitamins

- Minerals

- Water

- Natural fats and oils

This chapter tells you about these five nutrients, why they are good for your brain, what foods contain them, and how to make eating them more fun!

# AMINO ACIDS

All day long, your brain makes a substance called *protein*. It makes more than 30 different types of proteins—it's basically a protein factory. It builds them by hooking together nutrients called *amino acids.* Have you ever made a necklace by stringing beads together? That's basically how your brain puts together amino acids to make proteins. If your brain has LOTS of amino acids to make proteins with, it can do a much better job. This affects just about everything it does, including handling messages from your sense organs!

There are two ways to give your brain lots of amino acids. One is to eat a food rich in proteins as part of every meal. The other is to have a snack of a food with protein in it between meals. When your body digests the protein, it will take the amino acids and send them to your brain!

Foods that have a lot of protein in them are vegetables, eggs, seeds, cheese, yogurt, milk, meat, fish, seafood, wild game (such as deer or elk), poultry, nuts, and nut butters. "Tree nut" butters, like almond butter and pistachio butter, are better for you than peanut butter. Peanuts don't grow on trees, they grow underground! Tiny plants that grow in the ocean and lakes, called *algae,* also have a lot of protein in them, and seaweed does, too. Algae and seaweed can be grown in special containers of water and then turned into green powder to put into pills. You can get algae pills in bottles at health-food stores. The green powder has a mild taste that goes well with apple juice, so you can make a great protein-fruit smoothie with it!

## SO, HERE IS WHAT A DAY FULL OF GOOD AMINO ACIDS WOULD LOOK LIKE:

1. Breakfast with a protein food in it

2. A snack (2 hours later) with a protein food in it

3. Lunch (2 hours later) with a protein food in it

4. An afternoon snack (3 hours later) with a protein food in it

5. Dinner (2 hours later) with a protein food in it

6. A bedtime snack with a protein food in it.

To help you learn how to eat a protein food with each meal and snack, here's a list of some foods you could have with each meal. You can mix and match them any way you want! Just because I've suggested it under "lunch foods" doesn't mean you couldn't eat it for a snack, too. Packing a lunch or taking snacks with you when you leave home is always a good idea, too, so you'll have something good to eat when you need it! You can also get great ideas from cookbooks.

## SOME BREAKFAST FOODS WITH PROTEIN:

■ Eggs (scrambled, poached, fried, or hard-boiled)

■ Yogurt

■ Cereal made from oats or wheat

■ Almond butter on toast

■ An apple or banana with cashew butter

■ A glass of milk

- Cottage cheese with fruit
- A protein smoothie
- Breakfast meat or fish (but not bacon)

## SOME SNACK FOODS WITH PROTEIN:

- Sunflower or pumpkin seeds
- Cheese
- A hard-boiled egg
- Shrimp with cocktail sauce
- Cottage cheese
- Sliced vegetables with dip
- Trail mix
- Yogurt
- A banana with cashew butter
- Celery sticks with almond butter and raisins
- Nuts such as almonds, cashews, Brazil nuts, macadamias, walnuts, pistachios, or filberts

## SOME LUNCH FOODS WITH PROTEIN:

- Pasta with cheese or meat sauce
- A pistachio-butter sandwich
- Chicken and vegetables
- Beans with cheese
- A sandwich made with meat, fish, or poultry
- A glass of milk

- Vegetables with dip
- Soup or stew with meat and vegetables in it
- Yogurt
- Tacos with lots of meat in them

### SOME DINNER FOODS
### WITH PROTEIN:

- Fish, meat, turkey, or chicken as the main dish
- Meat or chicken with vegetables
- Vegetable lasagna with cheese on it
- Ground-beef patty with cheese
- Vegetables or mushrooms as the main or side dish
- A stir-fry with vegetables and meat or chicken in it
- Ground beef, as in a sloppy joe or stuffed peppers
- Pasta or pizza with meat sauce

Eating foods with protein is very important. Do you think you could try some of the things listed here? I'll bet you can! Remember to tell your parent and OT if you notice any changes when you eat more of these protein-rich foods.

# VITAMINS AND MINERALS

In order to work properly, your brain needs EVERY vitamin, and lots of it. The bosses of vitamins are minerals. Minerals tell the vitamins what to do and where to go in your brain. Without minerals, the vitamins can't be used by your brain! So minerals are important, too. Your brain wants each small bit of mineral to be gift wrapped by two amino acids. When amino acids wrap up minerals, it's called "chelation" (pronounced kee-LAY-shun). The best minerals to feed your brain are "chelated" minerals. If your parent buys minerals, the label on the bottle should say "chelated."

Foods with lots of vitamins and minerals are meat, vegetables, fruit, nuts, seeds, seaweeds, and algae. Your parent can also buy vitamins and minerals for you that come in different forms, such as liquids, pills, and capsules.

## WATER

Your brain needs a lot of water to help it get rid of waste and to keep its temperature correct. If you drink a glass of water every 2 hours each day, you will probably be giving your brain the amount of water it needs. Kids should drink 8 ounces of water at a time, which is the size of a regular measuring cup, every 2 hours. Adults should drink 12 ounces (a cup and a half) every 2 hours. The more pure the water is, the better. Water that comes from a well or has gone through a filter is great to drink.

If you don't enjoy drinking water, try different temperatures of water, including water with ice cubes in the glass. You could also drink fruit juice (with water added in), lemonade (with extra water added in), herbal teas, or vegetable juice. Watermelon and fresh pineapple have lots of water in them, too. A fun way to get more water is to make a homemade fruit pop. Pour some fruit juice in a paper cup, freeze it, and put a craft stick in the cup as it freezes. In about an hour, you've got a tasty, fruity treat!

"Drink a glass of water every 2 hours each day."

## NATURAL FATS AND OILS

Most of your brain's nerve cells are made of fat, so your brain has a lot of fat cells it has to help throughout the day. The way it helps them is to use parts of fat, called "fatty acids." Your body makes some of these fatty acids, but your brain must also get some from plants. The ones it gets from plants have a special name—"essential fatty acids." It is "essential" that you eat them every day, because your body can't make them on its own.

These essential fatty acids are found in all plants, and they can help your brain the most if the food isn't cooked very much. Raw plants, like the vegetables in a salad, or a piece of fresh fruit, are great for giving your brain those essential fatty acids. Plants that are cooked a little, as when stir-fried or steamed for a few minutes, still have lots of fatty acids left in them. Foods that are microwaved will lose too many of their fatty acids too fast and won't be able to help your brain as much.

Plants that have super-high amounts of fatty acids always have lots of natural fats and oils in them. The best plants are those that are raw, so rich sources include salads, fresh fruits and vegetables, fruits and vegetables that haven't been cooked very much, raw nuts (like walnuts, cashews, pecans, and filberts), seeds, seed oils (like coconut oil, corn oil, and sesame oil), plant oils (like olive oil), seaweeds, algae, and fish oil.

### HERE ARE SOME FOODS WITH LOTS OF FATTY ACIDS.

*See if you can eat some of these every day!*

- Avocados and guacamole
- Olive oil
- Raw pistachios, walnuts, Brazil nuts, pine nuts, pecans, and cashews
- Pumpkin and sunflower seeds (Ask your parent to put raw ones in a 350° oven and roast them for 5 minutes. Yummy!)
- Olives
- Spinach and kale (and other dark, leafy greens)
- Flaxseed meal, flax seeds (soaked overnight), and flax oil you can put on cereal, bread, toast, and salads
- Salmon, halibut, or cod
- Shrimp

You may have noticed that some of these foods also have protein in them! Eating these foods is a good way to give your brain fatty acids and proteins at the same time.

## IDEAS FOR MEALTIMES

Now you have a better idea of what to eat every day. Eating foods that give your brain what it needs is not only very smart, but fun, too! You can get some more ideas from cookbooks written for kids. Here are some ways to make eating even more fun.

## Make It Look Pretty

Why not make the food you eat more fun to look at on the plate? Try changing its shape, color, or position on the plate. Think of ways to take any food that comes in a package out of its package before it gets to the table. Cottage cheese, for example, is much more fun to eat when it is scooped into the middle of a pear half than if you eat it right out of the carton it comes in!

Speaking of color, did you know that the "dyes" used to give color to some foods and drinks are actually made from really yucky stuff—like petroleum—and can actually make sensory problems worse? You can read the labels of foods and avoid eating them if the label shows a number after the color, like "yellow 5." Food looks pretty just the way it is, without needing any dyes in it. You want to be eating food, not dyes. Some foods also have fake flavors added to them, which are also made out of yucky petroleum. Ask your parent to help you avoid such foods if you and your parent think that petroleum getting into your brain can make it overreact.

## Organic Foods

When you're helping your parent do the shopping at the grocery store, ask your parent to buy *organic foods* if possible. Organic foods are made or grown naturally, without using pesticides (bug chemicals), unnatural fertilizers, or sewage sludge (ew!). "Organic" also means that the food was not made by using additives. (Additives are the chemicals that can cause your senses to overreact.)

## Try new Foods

There are so many delicious foods out there that I bet you haven't even tried yet. Maybe your family can get involved in trying new foods together! Eating one new food each week is a great way to do it. At a meeting (such as the "Family Council Meeting" discussed in chapter 10), your family can decide which new food to try each week. Maybe each family member can fix one dish for the family each week, or at least help prepare one dish!

If you just can't stand a food that your parent wants you to try, ask permission to eat just one bite. The next time that food is served, take two bites. The following time, take three bites! Another thing to do is agree with your parent that you will eat some other food that has about the same nutrition in it, instead.

## Change the Utensils

If your bowl keeps slipping, use a nonskid placemat or one with tiny suction cups on the back. If you have trouble getting the food onto your fork, use a small piece of bread to push it on with. A plate with ribs that divide it into three parts, like the plastic ones used for a picnic, is great to eat off of at home, too. Sometimes asking for a smaller fork or spoon would help. If you are bothered by too much noise during meals, maybe your parent can arrange to have soft music playing and a tablecloth on the table, with plastic plates, forks, and spoons. This way, your meal will be much more quiet. If you turn off the TV during all meals, you will learn to enjoy your food better.

## Get Creative

Why not have a make-believe picnic in a different location in your home once in a while? Or, you can have a "circus minute" during the meal, where everyone makes a funny noise and a silly face. This is great fun, but it needs to be only a minute long! Maybe you can have a special meal with cartoon or super-hero plates and cups, cute napkins, and bright colors. How about putting a dif-  ferent person in charge of what your family talks about during the meal? You can talk about what each person did during the day, who would like to do what this weekend, and who would like to try a new food. Other ideas can be learning a new word together from a dictionary or learning some fun facts from an almanac or the newspaper.

## KEEP A "WHAT-I-ATE" DIARY

Sometimes eating a certain food will help your brain so much that you will feel extra good and very alert and awake, or you'll notice that things don't bother you so much from your senses. Or, a food might end up not helping your brain at all, or you would overreact to your senses even more after eating it. A great idea is to keep your very own personal diary where you can write down what you ate, and also what you noticed about yourself in the first hour after eating it. If you keep a "What-I-Ate" diary, you can figure out which foods actually help your brain the most, which foods seem to not make a difference, and which foods seem to make things worse for you. All you need is a few sheets of paper. Just write down everything you ate, then an hour later write down what you noticed about yourself in that hour. Did you feel good? Bad? Focused? Distracted? Hyper? Bothered? Calmer? Sleepy? Alert? Calm? Happy? You may notice that after eating certain foods, you almost always feel a certain way.

## DO IT!

Eating the right foods is very important and will help your brain learn to not overreact to your senses. Ask your parent to let you help buy some of the food items we talked about, if you don't have them in your home already.

We've gone over many new and different ways to get good nutrition. Getting good sleep is also important, and that is what the next chapter is about!

# CHAPTER 9

# Get Good Sleep

─────────── Did You Know? ───────────

You need 9 to 10 hours of sleep, every night. If you don't get enough sleep, you are much more likely to overreact to messages from your sense organs!

If you don't get enough sleep, you are grumpy the next day. Things bother you more, including messages from your senses. If bright lights bother you at school most days, then if you get only 4 hours of sleep, the next day those lights at school will bother you a WHOLE LOT MORE. So getting enough sleep is very important if you want your brain to stop overreacting to the messages from your senses.

## GET ENOUGH SLEEP

Try to get to sleep within 20 minutes of going to bed. The correct amount of sleep for you to get each night is

> *"Always aim for getting 9 or more hours of sleep every night, no matter what."*

between 9 and 10 hours. If you go to bed at 9 o'clock at night and get up at 7 o'clock in the morning, that's 10 hours of sleep. The best plan is to have a regular time for going to bed. Try to do all your bedtime activities in the same way and at the same time every evening. If you get tired too early, it's okay to go to bed early. It's okay if you wake up once or twice during the night, too.

On school days, go to bed at the correct time so you can get up on time for school the next day. Some kids want to stay up late to play computer games or watch a movie or TV, but then they don't get enough sleep. At school the next day, they overreact to their senses and don't enjoy school.

When you plan your bedtime, you should also plan to get everything else done *first*. For example, if you practice a musical instrument and read for 10 minutes every night, don't wait until bedtime to start doing those things—finish doing them *before* it's time to start getting ready for bed.

## MAKE YOUR BED COMFY

To make your mattress more stiff, put a wooden board between your box spring and your mattress. Or, put your mattress on the floor, and sleep there. You can even put an extra mattress on the floor if you might roll off your bed during the night. Ask for an extra pillow or blanket if having them would make your bed more comfortable. To prevent having to get up for a drink of water in the middle of the night, put a full glass of water next to your bed!

## SAY "GOOD NIGHT"

There are many ways to say "good night." The most important way is one that makes the adults who care for you remember how much you love them. Say "good night" with a smile, a hug, and giving or getting a kiss on the cheek. Talk about the good things that happened today, and what will happen tomorrow. If your parent wants to tell you a story, ask for one that is short and not scary.

## USE TOUCH TO FALL ASLEEP

*"Tucking you in should not take a long time—it should last only a few minutes."*

If a little bit of pressure on your skin calms you, try sleeping in a sleeping bag or under a heavy quilt. Cooling your bedroom with an air conditioner or fan will make you feel even calmer. Another way your sense of touch can help you is to take a shower or bath before bedtime. Your parent can also help you relax by giving you a foot massage or a foot bath, a back or tummy rub, or an arm or leg rub.

If you have spelling words to learn that week, when you lie down in your bed, your parent can print them on your back with a fingertip but spell them wrong on purpose. You can say the correct spelling. Playing this game will even help you learn your spelling words better! Your pajamas should not be too tight or too loose. They should not be lumpy or scratchy or have elastic cuffs that squeeze your skin too much. For an extra-special way to get ready for bed, ask your parent to put them in the clothes dryer for 2 minutes before you put them on. Sometimes you might even sleep better in the clothes you will wear in the morning, if your parent says it's okay.

*"Another way your sense of **touch** can **help** you get to **sleep** is to take a **shower** or **bath** before bedtime."*

## USE MOVEMENT TO FALL ASLEEP

About an hour before you go to bed, do about 4 minutes of a movement you enjoy doing. This way, you're giving your muscles a reason to get tired over the next hour, so that you feel more relaxed at bedtime. For example, you can do a little dance, ride a bike, do some jumping jacks, take a short walk, go up and down the stairs, or shoot baskets. What you do isn't as important as enjoying it and doing it for only 4 minutes. If you didn't get any exercise during the day, it's okay to do it for longer than 4 minutes!

## USE SIGHT TO FALL ASLEEP

To get calm while you're lying in bed and trying to go to sleep, look at something that has many slowly changing or moving colors. A lava light or fiber-optic lamp is a good idea. Having two lamps that change colors is even better, because you can have one on both sides of your bed! That way, no matter which way you turn, you always have a fun light display to look at. Looking at a lighted aquarium or one with plastic fish and fake water that you plug in will also help you get to sleep. A Christmas-tree color wheel that throws red, green, yellow, and blue light onto your bedroom wall also works well.

*"a lava light with a glob of color that keeps changing is great."*

Another way to use vision to help you get to sleep is to sit at your desk or in a comfy chair and do a crossword puzzle, a dot-to-dot game, or a sudoku puzzle. Or, you could color in a coloring book or play a game in a book full of games and puzzles for a few minutes. Doing any kind of needlecraft (like cross-stitching or crochet) is also great for calming yourself down at bedtime.

If you want a night-light, ask for a dimmer switch so you can control how bright it gets. Regular bulbs are better than fluorescent bulbs for your bedroom. If the light from outside your window keeps you awake, hang canvas or a dark sheet over your window to block it out.

## LISTEN TO FALL ASLEEP

If noises around your home keep you awake at bedtime, ask your parent to put corkboard on your walls or heavy curtains in your room. Then, you can create "white noise" in your bedroom by plugging in a white-noise machine, an aquarium with an air pump or filter, a fan, an air purifier, a CD of nature sounds, or "low, slow, and no" music. Maybe you can sleep in a bedroom that is far away from where the noise comes from in your home.

Another way to calm down at bedtime is to listen to a CD that helps you relax, such as "Quiet Time."

## HAVE A PROTEIN SNACK

About 30 minutes before you go to bed, eat a small snack with a high-protein food in it. The correct amount is what you can hold in your cupped hand (fingers bent and touching together on the sides). A small amount of bread or toast is okay, as long as the high-protein food is also part of the snack, like some cashew butter or some cheese. A small bowl of oatmeal works great.

## IF YOU GRIND YOUR TEETH

If you grind your teeth while you sleep, your brain probably isn't getting enough of the minerals it needs. Ask your parent to get the advice of a professional who knows about nutrition. That person will probably advise that you take some chelated minerals every day.

## IF YOU SWEAT

If you sweat a lot while you sleep, your brain probably isn't getting enough water or enough of the fatty acids it needs. Ask your parent to get the advice of a professional who knows about nutrition. That person will probably advise that you drink more water and maybe swallow a fish-oil capsule with every meal, so your brain can get more fatty acids.

# IF YOU CAN'T WAKE UP

Even if you get 9 hours of sleep, you might have trouble waking up in the morning. If you have this problem, use a different way to wake yourself up. Here are a few ideas.

## Alarm Clock Tricks

Ask your parent to buy an alarm clock with a real bell on the top. If that kind of alarm clock isn't loud enough to wake you up, you can make it even louder. You can put it inside a metal cookie box (the kind that has a metal lid) that is set on its side, without the lid. Another idea is to put it on a metal pie pan that has dimes laid all over it. The dimes are small and light, so they jump a little bit and make a tinkle sound that helps wake you up.

## Shake Yourself Awake!

Ask your parent to go online to a Web site for people with hearing problems and buy a timed vibrator. Then you can set it for when you want to wake up, just like an alarm clock—only the vibrator doesn't ring. You put it under your mattress when you go to bed. When morning comes, it starts vibrating, but the vibrations keep getting bigger and bigger, so you wake up at the right time because your body feels the vibrations in your mattress.

## Watery Wake-Up

Ask your parent to wake you up by wiping your forehead or cheeks with water that is a pleasant temperature for you to feel. Before you go to bed, use the bathroom sink to show your parent the temperature you want the water to be.

## IF YOU WAKE UP GRUMPY OR SPACEY

Most kids wake up happy, smiling, and refreshed in the morning. But what if you get 9 hours of sleep and when you wake up in the morning, you feel bothered right away? Maybe you frown, say mean things, act sassy, or argue. Maybe you complain about the light being bright or your pajamas feeling yucky. Ask your parent whether you tend to be extra grumpy in the morning. Another thing to ask about is whether you have trouble figuring things out, whether you take a very long time to do things that should only take a little bit of time to do, or whether you seem spacey and forgetful.

If you are grumpy or spacey for about the first 30 minutes after you wake up in the morning, your brain probably isn't getting enough of the amino acids it needs. Ask your parent to get the advice of a professional who knows about nutrition. That person will probably advise that you eat more protein. You can always eat a slightly bigger protein snack at bedtime. In the morning, you can even start right away by drinking a protein smoothie or a protein blender drink. There are many great recipes for those, and they taste great!

# DO IT!

Getting enough sleep can help you learn not to overreact to your senses. We've talked about ways to help you get to sleep, and how to get the right amount of sleep. Now you just have to do your part to make sure you get good sleep. You'll be glad you did!

Protecting your brain from stress chemicals is also important, and that is what the last chapter is about.

*"In the morning, you can **drink a** protein smoothie or a protein blender drink."*

# CHAPTER 10

# Take Good Care of Yourself

When you are under too much stress, some stress glands in your body put chemicals into your blood, and your blood takes those chemicals to your brain! The stress chemicals get in the way of your brain making the proteins it is supposed to be making, and you end up overreacting to your senses.

Stress can come in many different ways. For some kids, a stressful event can be having to take a test at school, having to stop playing a computer game because it's bedtime, or arguing with a friend. For others, a stressful event might be having to stand up in front of the class to give a talk, having to eat a food that is new, or being tickled. There are hundreds of different events that a person might find stressful, including any kind of overreacting to your senses.

# KEEP STRESS AT BAY

The more stresses you have to cope with, the more likely you are to overreact to your senses. One way to not overreact is to prevent stresses from building up in your life. Here are some suggestions. Which ones do you think you could start doing, or do more of?

## Get More Active

Hobbies that allow you to create things are great. Maybe you could try cooking new foods, doing needlecraft, drawing, coloring, or working with clay. Going somewhere once each week to get strong exercise is also a good idea. You could try swimming, dance, or bowling, for example.

## Meet with Your Parent

A great practice is to have a regular time, once every month, to sit down and talk with your parent about everything happening in your life. This special meeting is known as a Personal Private Interview, or PPI. It is called that because it is all three. It is *personal* between you and your parent, it is held *in private* when nobody else is around, and it is an *interview* where both of you talk with each other. This meeting would be a good time to talk about a stressful event that's coming up. Have your PPI in your bedroom, and mark it on the calendar so both of you remember to have it every month. During the month, write down anything you want to talk about, so you have it ready for your meeting.

## Meet as a Family

In addition to meeting privately with you, maybe your parent can arrange a regular meeting of the family, to be held once each week. This Family Council meeting is a great time to discuss any problems your family members are having. It is also a good time for allowances to be given, if you get one. You can discuss what your family can do to prepare for an upcoming weekend, holiday, or vacation. You can also include a game, a song, or a special dessert just for fun. Having a regular Family Council meeting helps prevent stress for everyone!

## Replace Your Fear

One of the best ways to have less stress in your life is to get really good at choosing caution instead of fear as your way of dealing with things that are hard. There is nothing wrong with seeing that something is going to be hard to do or that it might cause you stress. But you always have a choice. You can choose to have fear about it, or you can have *caution,* instead.

> *"The more stresses you have to cope with, the more likely you are to overreact to your senses."*

| FEAR | CAUTION |
|------|---------|
| I can't take action | I can take action |
| Makes more danger and stress | Makes less danger and stress |
| I can't do this | I can do this |
| I worry more | I worr$\bar{y}$ less |
| I want to run away from it | I can handle it |
| I don't know enough | I can learn more (read a book about it) |
| Things are awful | Things are stressful, but not awful |
| I can't control what happens | I can help control what happens |

"You always have a choice. You can choose to have fear about it, or you can have caution, instead."

If you choose fear, you will think that you are trapped and helpless. You'll think that you can't handle the stress, and you'll worry a lot. You'll want to run away from the stress and won't learn much about how to deal with it. You'll believe that things are just awful. When this happens, you're likely to overreact to your senses, also.

If you choose *caution,* you will realize that you can help control what happens and that you're not trapped, after all. You'll know that you can handle the stress, and you won't worry about it. You'll want to go *toward* the stress and *learn more about it,* rather than run away from it. You'll recognize that things are stressful, but not awful. You will also probably not overreact to your senses!

"If you choose caution, you will realize that you can help control what happens and that you're not trapped, after all."

## WHICH OF THESE KIDS WOULD YOU RATHER BE LIKE FOR YOUR ENTIRE LIFE— CAUTIOUS CARRIE OR FEARFUL FRANK?

## Cautious Carrie ———— and Fearful Frank ————

Cautious Carrie and Fearful Frank went on a field trip to the zoo with their entire class. At the zoo, the animal trainer invited all of the students to come to the snake area. He held a huge python in a careful way and talked about snakes, how to avoid getting bitten by them, what they eat, and how their skin is not slimy. Then he invited everyone to come up, one at a time, and touch the python so they could feel that it isn't slimy and see what the python's thick muscles feel like.

Fearful Frank secretly wanted to run away from the snake area. He didn't want to learn anything about snakes or pythons. He worried that the python would bite or squeeze him to death if he came anywhere near it. He worried that he would end up touching it in a wrong way that would make the python attack him. He feared that

there was nothing he could ever do to be safe around any snake. He was very unhappy during the snake time, and he had very high stress. He overreacted to his senses, too, saying that it was too hot, the sun was too bright, the wind was blowing too much, his shirt felt scratchy, and the animal sounds at the zoo were too loud.

Cautious Carrie, however, went right into the snake area with the class. She was willing to go near the snake and touch it, and she wanted to hear the directions from the trainer about how to touch the python the right way. She wanted to listen to the trainer about how to handle snakes and what to do if she came across one in her yard or out in a field somewhere. She was happy at snake time and had no stress. She enjoyed learning about snakes and touching the python when it was her turn. And she did not overreact to any of her senses.

If you choose caution over fear, you will have MUCH LESS STRESS in your life. Almost every day, you have a chance to practice this skill. *Always* choose caution over fear.

---

## WHAT TO DO BEFORE, DURING, AND AFTER A STRESSFUL EVENT

Remember the quizzes about what bothers you with your various senses? Whenever you overreact, you are having a stressful event. Maybe you know you will be in a place that might be stressful for you, such as a loud crowd or a room with flickering lights. Or, maybe you'll be doing an activity that you find stressful, such as being spun around, eating a meal with new foods, or feeling scratchy cloth on your skin. It could be that a big event like a ball game, a class trip, a bus ride, a birthday party, or an amusement park visit is stressful for you. Whatever kinds of events cause stress for you, it is important to be ready when stress comes. The way to be ready involves knowing three things:

1. What to do BEFORE it happens, to get ready for it

2. What to do WHEN it is happening, to stay as calm as you can

3. What to do AFTER it happens, to get calm again

Most of the really good ways to have less stress can be done at all three times. You might want to do some of them before, some of them during, and some of them after a stressful event. Do these at the best times for you, to help you the most.

## BEFORE THE EVENT
### Do a Warm-Up Activity

To calm down in the few minutes before a stressful event, try some sort of warm-up or practice activity, just as a baseball player takes practice swings before going to bat. Sometimes movement, like doing something constructive with your hands, helps get you ready to face stress better. You can play with clay, crazy putty, modeling compound, or a balloon filled with sand.

## Get Relaxed

Staying calm helps you think and plan better when it comes to handling stress. One way to relax better is to think about being in a favorite place or floating on an air mattress on a calm pool or pond. Think about staying calm and handling the stressful event well. Another way is to take four or five slow, deep breaths while you relax, each breath taking about 5 seconds in and 5 seconds out. Sometimes you can relax better by playing a CD that guides you, like "Quiet Time."

You can sometimes use touch to help you relax. Maybe you calm down better right after you take a bath, hug a Teddy bear, suck on some ice, or play with your rubber-band "giant octopus" (from chapter 4). If you can hold and stroke a friendly pet, that's also a good way to relax!

## Use Music

Listen to music with words that help you feel better. Music that goes along with poetry, such as in a hymn, is often good for helping you get ready to face stress. Listening to music you enjoy or playing a musical instrument can also help.

# DURING THE EVENT
## Help Control What Happens

Maybe you can help control what will happen during the stressful event. See if you can be allowed to stop the event if it bothers you too much, or at least take a break from it. Maybe you can ask the adults to talk with you ahead of time about any changes that could arise, so nothing comes as a surprise. If you have a choice, maybe you can even walk away from the stressful event.

*"Always choose caution over fear."*

## Use Wise Self-Talk

When you are in a room where stress occurred for you in the past, be extra careful about staying calm. Tell yourself, "I will stay in control," "I can handle this," and "I will stay calm." Instead of being afraid of what will happen, tell yourself to use caution about what will happen.

## Think of Other Things

Sometimes you can be in a stressful event and not have to pay attention to it, like when you're taking a long ride on an elevator or escalator or flying somewhere in an airplane. Try to arrange to have a fun book to read or color in. Listen to a CD with a story or music. Play a hand-held computer game.

# AFTER THE EVENT
## Have a Calming-Down Place

Try to arrange a place where you can take a safe "time-out" when you are feeling stress. It should be a private area that is not going to upset you. It should have a nice place to sit where you can relax, such as a beanbag chair or a pile of pillows. The light should not be bright. If you are calmer when you are holding something, have a small piece of yarn or a soft cloth. Rocking in a rocking chair or porch swing can be calming, too.

## Talk about It

One of the neat things about having friends is that you can talk with them about almost anything, including your stressful event. Maybe you could write a poem or song about it. Talk about the strong points, or "good news," about how you handled the stressful event. Even if you don't think you did very well, you can still learn from what happened, so next time can be better.

## Dump off Strong Feelings

Don't try to hold in or hide strong feelings, such as anger or being very sad. Punch a punching bag, run around a safe path, do jumping jacks, pull weeds, or pull leaves off of bushes. If you want to pull leaves, first be sure it's okay with whoever owns the bushes! Ride a bicycle, take a walk, or use your hands to play with clay, modeling compound, or finger-paints.

## Pamper Yourself

Dealing with stress takes your energy away and makes you feel tired. After a stressful event, give yourself some calming-down time. What calms you might not work for all other kids, so pick activities that work best for you. Maybe you would like to take a nap or lie down in a sleeping bag or on a sofa. Maybe you could listen to a CD. If you enjoy taking a shower or bath, why not take one after a stressful event? Getting some hugs from your parent or wrapping yourself up in a blanket might help, too. Taking a few deep, slow breaths is another way to get calm. The important thing is that you learn what calms you down best, and you can arrange for that to happen after the stressful event.

*"Often your sense of movement can help you with strong feelings."*

## Celebrate

Arrange to do something fun after a stressful event. Celebrate your success at dealing with the stress. Maybe you can do an activity you like or have a special treat. Maybe your parent can give you a chore-free day or a long back rub!

# A FINAL WORD

Now you know how to help your brain handle sense messages better by getting enough sleep, eating the right foods, avoiding outside chemicals, and keeping your stress level low. We've also talked about many fun ways to train your brain to stop overreacting to your senses. Be sure to talk with your parent or your OT about any ideas in this book that you think might help you. Go ahead and use these techniques to get along better with your senses.

## You Can Do It!

# Glossary

**Additives**—Additives are chemicals added to foods and drinks, mainly to make them look or taste better. Most additives are petroleum based and can cause sensory overreaction, so you want to avoid them. There are more than 6,000 types of additives in food and drinks! Try to eat organic foods if possible. Also see the entries for "Overreaction" and "Organic."

**Amino acid**—This is a material that is used to make proteins in your body. The brain needs several amino acids every day. Also see the entry for "Protein."

**Brain food**—Brain food is food that contains nutrients needed by your brain. Also see the entry for "Nutrients."

**Brain Gym**—Brain Gym is a program of easy, fun movements for various body parts. You can find out more at *www.braingym.com*.

**Chelated minerals**—These are special minerals that are bonded with amino acids. When minerals are chelated, your brain can absorb them and use them more easily than unchelated ones. Without minerals, your brain can't use the vitamins you eat! Chelated minerals are very important. Also see the entry for "Minerals."

**Developmental optometrist**—This is an eye doctor who knows a lot about helping you with "close vision," or seeing things within a few inches of your eyes. A developmental optometrist will usually provide vision therapy if you need it. Also see the entries for "Optometrist" and "Vision therapy."

**Distraction**—Having your attention taken away from something you want to pay attention to.

**Essential fatty acids**—These are fatty acids your body needs, which it can't make on its own. So, you must eat them instead. Eating plants, like vegetables in a salad, or a piece of fresh fruit, gives your brain essential fatty acids. Raw plants are best—try eating more salads, fresh fruits and vegetables, fruits and vegetables that haven't been cooked very much, raw nuts (like walnuts, cashews, pecans, and filberts), seeds, seed oils (like coconut oil, corn oil, and sesame oil), plant oils (like olive oil), seaweeds, algae, and fish oil. Also see the entry for "Fatty acids."

**Family Council meeting**—This is a regular meeting of family members to discuss issues in the family or with individual members, such as allowances, plans for holidays and weekends, and reviewing schedules and activities.

**Fatty acids**—Fatty acids make up the fats that your brain needs. They are found in natural food oils and fats. They help your brain and body use the vitamins needed to function every day, such as vitamin A, vitamin D, vitamin E, and vitamin K. They also help your brain process sensory messages. See the entry for "Vitamins."

**Fluorescent light**—A fluorescent light is a glass tube with a coating on the inner wall that glows when the light is turned on. People who overreact to vision sometimes notice that fluorescent lights are too bright or too blue, that they flicker, and that they cause headaches and migraines.

**Hypoallergenic**—This means something is unlikely to cause an allergic reaction, because it doesn't have any materials in it that people tend to be allergic to.

**Minerals**—A mineral is a natural substance that is not an animal or a vegetable, but it has a special chemical makeup. The human body needs several minerals every day. Minerals tell the vitamins you eat what to do and where to go in your brain!

**Nutrient**—A nutrient is a part of a food or drink that supports and sustains life and growth. Vitamins, minerals, fatty acids, amino acids, and water are all nutrients. Also see the entry for "Nutrition."

**Nutrition**—A living thing uses nutrients to grow, and we call this process "nutrition." The purpose of eating and drinking is to give your brain and body nutrients. Also see the entry for "nutrient."

**Occupational therapist**—This is a person who has special training in how to help children control body parts, muscles, and senses. An "OT" uses body-movement activities to help a person's body function better—and feel better, too!

**Optometrist**—This is an eye doctor who gives eye exams and can help you get glasses if you need them. Also see the entry for "Developmental optometrist."

**Organic**—This is a label for foods (and fabrics) that are made or grown without using pesticides (bug chemicals), unnatural fertilizers, or sewage sludge. "Organic" also means that the food was not made by using additives, which are chemicals made out of petroleum. Additives are used to change the look or the taste of food (such as "dyes," which are sometimes used to turn food a different color). Also see the entry for "Additives."

**OT**—A short term for "occupational therapist." Also see the entry for "Occupational therapist."

**Overreaction**—An overreaction is when the brain reacts too much to sensory messages it gets from a sense organ. You can help your brain stop over-reacting by giving it the right foods and enough sleep, by doing special exercises, and by avoiding stress chemicals and outside chemicals. Also see the entry for "Sense."

**Personal Private Interview**—This is a personal conversation you have with your parent or with your teacher on a regular basis. In your Personal Private Interview, you can talk about all kinds of things that are going on with you, and it's just between the two of you.

**Physical therapist**—This is a person who has special training in helping you if you have sensory issues of the muscles and your moving body parts, such as your arms and legs.

**Physician**—This is a doctor who can diagnose a disease and decide the best way to treat it.

**Protein**— A protein is something your brain makes by hooking together nutrients called *amino acids.* If your brain has lots of amino acids to make proteins with, it works much better. This affects just about everything it does—including handling messages from your sense organs. Proteins are necessary for all living creatures—and your brain makes more than 30 of them! Also see the entry for "Amino acids."

**Rebounder**—A small, portable trampoline.

**Sensory**—"Sensory" has to do with your awareness of your senses—like hearing, smell, taste, vision, touch, muscle movement, and feelings inside your body, such as hunger.

**Speech and language therapist**—This is a person who is trained in sensory issues inside and around the mouth, including the ability to speak and eat.

**Therapy ball**—A large, sturdy rubber ball that you can sit on, lie on, or have someone roll over you with pressure.

**T-stool**—A large stool made out of a seat with only one leg. It looks like a giant thumbtack and allows a little bit of movement when you sit on it.

**Velcro**—A type of fabric that sticks together and is pretty strong. It comes in two pieces—hooks on one piece latch onto little loops on the other piece.

**Vision therapy**—A set of eye exercises given by a developmental optometrist to help you control your eye muscles and read better. Also see the entry for "Developmental optometrist."

**Visual contrast**—This is how you tell two objects apart by looking at their color or shape.

**Visual focusing**—The ability to adjust your vision to do tasks up close to your eyes or far away from your eyes, as needed.

**Visual identifying**—Knowing the correct name or label for something when you see it.

**Visual tracking**—Following a moving object with your eyes and being able to focus on it the whole time.

**Vitamins**—Essential nutrients that occur naturally in plant and animal tissues. Several vitamins can't be made by the human body, so they must be eaten daily. The brain needs every vitamin.

**White noise**—A soft, ongoing sound that blocks out louder and less ongoing noises.

# Resources

These are some of the resources I personally recommend. There are hundreds of other resources available. I have listed the topics in approximately the same order as they occur in this book.

## Resources for Sensory Processing Disorder

1. *The Everything Parent's Guide to Sensory Integration Disorder,* by Terri Mauro. Avon, MA: F & W Media, 2006.

2. *Learning Games: Exploring the Senses through Play,* by Jackie Silberg. Beltsville, MD: Gryphon House, 2006.

3. *The Out-of-Sync Child: Recognizing and Coping with Sensory Processing Disorder* (revised edition), by Carol Kranowitz. New York, NY: Penguin, 2005.

4. *The Out-of-Sync Child Has Fun: Activities for Kids with Sensory Processing Disorder,* by Carol Kranowitz. New York, NY: Penguin, 2003.

5. *Parenting a Child with Sensory Processing Disorder,* by Christopher Auer and Susan Blumberg. Oakland, CA: New Harbinger, 2006.

6. *Raising a Sensory Smart Child: The Definitive Handbook for Helping Your Child with Sensory Processing Issues,* by Lindsey Biel and Nancy Peske. New York, NY: Penguin, 2009.

7. *Sensational Kids: Hope and Help for Children with Sensory Processing Disorder,* by Lucy Miller and Doris Fuller. New York, NY: Penguin, 2006.

8. *Sensory Secrets,* by Catherine Schneider. Siloam Springs, AR: Concerned Communications, 2001.

9. *Starting Sensory Therapy: Fun Activities That Won't Destroy Your Home!* by Bonnie Arnwine. Arlington, TX: Sensory World, 2011.

10. *Tools for Parents: A Handbook to Bring Sensory Integration into the Home,* by Diana Henry. Glendale, AZ: Henry OT Services, 2001.

11. *Tools for Tots: Sensory Strategies for Toddlers and Preschoolers,* by Diana Henry. Glendale, AZ: Henry OT Services, 2007.

12. *The Ultimate Guide to Sensory Processing Disorder,* by Roya Ostovar. Arlington, TX: Sensory World, 2010.

13. *Understanding Sensory Dysfunction*, by Polly Emmons and Liz Anderson. Philadelphia, PA: Jessica Kingsley, 2005.

## Resources for Sensory Treatment of Attention-Deficit Disorder

1. *ADD/ADHD: A Parent's Practical Guide,* by Marie Isom. Keaau, HI: Gigglepuss Press, 2002.

2. *ADD/ADHD Drug Free: Natural Alternatives and Practical Exercises to Help Your Child Focus,* by Frank Jacobelli and L. Watson. New York, NY: American Management Association, 2008.

3. *Helping Your ADD Child: Hundreds of Practical Solutions,* by John Taylor. Monmouth, OR: A.D.D. Plus, 2001.

4. *The Survival Guide for Kids with ADD or ADHD,* by John Taylor. Minneapolis, MN: Free Spirit, 2006.

5. *Victory over ADHD: A Holistic Approach to Helping Children with ADHD,* by Deborah Merlin. Summertown, TN: Healthy Living Publications, 2009.

## Resources for Autism Spectrum Disorder and Asperger Syndrome

1. *Children with Starving Brains: A Medical Treatment Guide for Autism Spectrum Disorder* (4th edition), by Jaquelyn McCandless. Putney, VT: Bramble Books, 2009.

2. *The Everything Parent's Guide to Children with Autism* (2nd edition), by Adelle Tilton. Avon, MA: Adams Media, 2010.

3. *My Child Has Autism: What Parents Need to Know,* by Clarissa Willis. Beltsville, MD: Gryphon House, 2009.

4. *Teaching Young Children with Autism Spectrum Disorder,* by Clarissa Willis. Beltsville, MD: Gryphon House, 2006.

5. *Understanding Asperger's Syndrome: Fast Facts,* by Emily Burrows and Sheila Wagner. Arlington, TX: Future Horizons, 2004.

## Resources for the Sense of Touch

1. *The Early Childhood Fun Express,* by Shirley Burdick and John Taylor. Monmouth, OR: A.D.D. Plus, 1995.

2. *Look What You Can Make with Dozens of Household Items!* by Kathy Ross and Hank Schneider. Honesdale, PA: Boyds Mills Press, 1998.

## Resources for the Sense of Movement

1. *Brain Gym: Simple Activities for Whole Brain Learning,* by Paul Dennison and Gail Dennison. Ventura, CA: Edu-Kinesthetics, 1986.

2. *The Early Childhood Fun Express,* by Shirley Burdick and John Taylor. Monmouth, OR: A.D.D. Plus, 1995.

3. *Fine Motor Fun,* by Sherrill Flora. Minneapolis, MN: Key Education, 2006.

4. *Gross Motor Fun,* by Michael Abraham. Minneapolis, MN: Key Education, 2008.

5. *Moving with a Purpose: Developing Programs for Preschoolers of All Abilities,* by Renee McCall and Diane Craft. Champaign, IL: Human Kinetics, 2000.

6. *125 Brain Games for Toddlers and Twos: Simple Games to Promote Early Brain Development,* by Jackie Silberg. Beltsville, MD: Gryphon House, 2000.

7. *The Out-of-Sync Child Has Fun: Activities for Kids with Sensory Processing Disorder,* by Carol Kranowitz. New York, NY: Perigee, 2006.

8. *Growing an In-Sync Child: Simple, Fun Activities to Help Every Child Develop, Learn and Grow,* by Carol Kranowitz and Joye Newman. New York, NY: Perigee, 2010.

9. *The Wiggle & Giggle Busy Book: 365 Fun, Physical Activities for Toddlers and Preschoolers,* by Trish Kuffner. New York, NY: Simon & Schuster, 2005.

10. *Wiggle, Giggle & Shake: 200 Ways to Move and Learn,* by Rae Pica. Beltsville, MD: Gryphon House, 2009.

## Resources for the Sense of Hearing

1. *Auditory Processes,* by Pamela Gillet. Novato, CA: Academic Therapy, 1993.

2. *Learning Process Skills,* by Stanley Riley. Novato, CA: Academic Therapy, 1992.

## Resources for the Sense of Vision

1. *Eyes on Track: A Missing Link to Successful Learning,* by Kristy Remick, Carol Stroud, and Vicki Bedes. Folsom, CA: JF's Publishing, 2000.

2. *Learning Process Skills,* by Stanley Riley. Novato, CA: Academic Therapy, 1992.

3. *Eyegames: Easy and Fun Visual Exercises—An OT and Optometrist Offer Activities to Enhance Vision!* by Lois Hickman and Rebecca Hutchins. Arlington, TX: Sensory World, 2010.

## Resources for the Senses of Taste and Smell

1. *How to Grow Fresh Air: 50 Houseplants That Purify Your Home or Office,* by B. Wolverton. New York, NY: Penguin, 1996.

2. *Just Take a Bite: Easy, Effective Answers to Food Aversions and Eating Challenges,* by Lori Ernsperger and Tania Stegen-Hanson. Arlington, TX: Future Horizons, 2004.

3. *Why Can't I Eat That! Helping Kids Obey Medical Diets,* by John Taylor and R.S. Latta. Monmouth, OR: A.D.D. Plus, 1996.

## Resources for Improving Brain Nutrition

1. *The A.D.D. Nutrition Solution,* by Marcia Zimmerman. New York, NY: Holt, 1999.

2. Assisting Brain Biochemistry: Dietary and Nutritional Treatment of A.D.D. [audio CD], by John Taylor. Monmouth, OR: A.D.D. Plus, 1998.

3. *Healthy Food for Healthy Kids: A Practical and Tasty Guide to Your Child's Nutrition,* by Bridget Swinney. New York, NY: Simon & Schuster, 1999.

4. *Nutrition & Attention Deficit Disorder: How to Use Nutrition as a Treatment Option,* by John Taylor. Monmouth, OR: A.D.D. Plus, 2006.

5. Nutrition and Neurochemistry: The ADD Link [DVD], by John Taylor. Monmouth, OR: A.D.D. Plus, 2006.

6. *Our Children Are What Our Children Eat,* by Laura Thompson. Encinitas, CA: America's House of Health, 2009.

7. *Special Diets for Special Kids,* by Lisa Lewis. Arlington, TX: Future Horizons, 1998.

8. *Special Diets for Special Kids Two,* by Lisa Lewis. Arlington, TX: Future Horizons, 2001.

## Resources for Improving Sleep

1. *Be the Boss of Your Sleep: Self-Care for Kids,* by Timothy Culbert and Rebecca Kajander. Minneapolis, MN: Free Spirit, 2007.

2. Quiet Time: Very Pleasant Relaxation Training for Children [audio CD], by John Taylor. Monmouth, OR: A.D.D. Plus, 1995.

## Resources for Improving Stress-Coping Skills

1. *Anger Control Training for Children & Teens: The Adult's Guidebook for Teaching Healthy Handling of Anger,* by John Taylor. Monmouth, OR: A.D.D. Plus, 1991.

2. *Be the Boss of Your Stress: Self-Care for Kids,* by Timothy Culbert and Rebwecca Kajander. Minneapolis, MN: Free Spirit, 2007.

3. Quiet Time: Very Pleasant Relaxation Training for Children [audio CD], by John Taylor. Monmouth, OR: A.D.D. Plus, 1995.

4. *The Relaxation & Stress Reduction Workbook for Kids,* by Lawrence Shapiro and Robin Sprague. Oakland, CA: New Harbinger, 2009.

5. *Stress Can Really Get on Your Nerves,* by Trevor Romain and Elizabeth Verdick. Minneapolis, MN: Free Spirit, 2000.

## Resources for Avoiding Toxic Chemical Exposures

1. *ADD/ADHD Drug Free: Natural Alternatives and Practical Exercises to Help Your Child Focus,* by Frank Jacobelli and L. Watson. New York, NY: American Management Association, 2008.

2. *The Beginner's Guide to Natural Living,* by Larry Cook. Summertown, TN: Healthy Living Publications, 2006.

3. *The Complete Idiot's Guide to Organic Living,* by Eliza Sarasohn and Sonia Weiss. New York, NY: Penguin, 2009.

4. *Diet, Toxins, ADHD & Behavior: The Effects of Toxic Chemical Exposure,* edited by John Taylor. Monmouth, OR: A.D.D. Plus, 2008.

5. *Healthier Food for Busy People,* by Jane Hersey. Alexandria, VA: Pear Tree Press, 2007.

6. *How to Grow Fresh Air: 50 Houseplants That Purify Your Home or Office,* by B. Wolverton. New York, NY: Penguin, 1996.

7. Nutrition & Neurochemistry: The A.D.D. Link [DVD], by John Taylor. Monmouth, OR: A.D.D. Plus, 2006.

8. *The Organic Food Guide: How to Shop Smarter and Eat Healthier,* by Steve Meyerowitz. Guilford, CT: Globe Pequot, 2004.

9. *Our Children Are What Our Children Eat,* by Laura Thompson. Encinitas, CA: America's House of Health, 2009.

10. *The Safe Shopper's Bible: A Consumer's Guide to Nontoxic Household Products, Cosmetics, and Food,* by David Steinman and Samuel Epstein. Hoboken, NJ: Wiley, 1995.

11. *Victory over ADHD: A Holistic Approach to Helping Children with ADHD,* by Deborah Merlin. Summertown, TN: Healthy Living Publications, 2009.

12. *Why Can't My Child Behave? Cope? Learn?* by Jane Hersey. Williamsburg, VA: Pear Tree Press, 2006.

## Resources for Help at School

1. Answers to A.D.D.: The School Success Tool Kit [DVD], by John Taylor. Monmouth, OR: A.D.D. Plus, 2006.

2. *The Attention Deficit/Hyperactive Student at School: Real Answers for Today's Classrooms,* by John Taylor. Monmouth, OR: A.D.D. Plus, 1992.

3. *Building Sensory Friendly Classrooms to Support Children with Challenging Behaviors: Implementing Data Driven Strategies!* by Rebecca Moyes. Arlington, TX: Sensory World, 2010.

4. *Learning Process Skills,* by Stanley Riley. Novato, CA: Academic Therapy, 1992.

5. *Sensory Integration: A Guide for Preschool Teachers,* by Christy Isbell and Rebecca Isbell. Beltsville, MD: Gryphon House, 2007.

6. *Sensory Integration: Practical Strategies and Sensory Motor Activities for Use in the Classroom,* by Michael Abraham. Greensboro, NC: Carson Dellosa, 2002.

7. *Teaching Young Children with Autism Spectrum Disorder,* by Clarissa Willis. Beltsville, MD: Gryphon House, 2006.

# A SPECIAL MESSAGE

# for the Occupational Therapist

*This book supports your role* as the lead therapist to desensitize the sensory-avoiding child or teen. I frequently mention that the reader is to "ask your OT" about whether an activity would be helpful. The activities are described in sufficient detail and with attractive titles to arouse the child's interest about doing them as part of treatment. They will hopefully become important and helpful components of the sensory therapeutic experience program, or STEP, or the sensory diet you are developing. While commonly called a "sensory diet," I like to refer to the STEP as more of a "sensory banquet," because of the connotations of abundance, joy, and choice in that term.

There is more to the story, however, when desensitizing a sensory avoider. This book acknowledges the importance of facilitating brain functioning, along with leading the child through sensory-banquet activities. The chapters on getting sufficient sleep, obtaining adequate brain nutrition, and maximizing stress-coping skills add important dimensions to the overall treatment plan. The fourth factor that often seems to affect symptom levels on a daily basis for sensory avoiders is the amount of interference in brain functioning caused by toxic chemical exposures that day. I introduce this factor in chapter 8. According to an ever-expanding wealth of scientific studies, it is especially important to guard against toxic exposures with children and teens who are on the autism spectrum or who have attention-deficit disorder (with or without hyperactivity).

In discussing the human senses, I have collapsed three senses into one: proprioception, kinesthesis, and balance. For simplicity, and to make this book more readable for the preadolescent reader, I refer to this combination of three senses as one sense—"movement." For an adolescent or a very mature child who wants to know more, there is nothing wrong with providing further information that treats these three senses as separate entities.

My intention is that this book will become the handiest tool you've ever had for working with sensory avoiders.

# A SPECIAL MESSAGE
# for the Teacher

*Because school can be a very challenging place* for a sensory-avoiding student, this book supports your role as an important contributor to the overall treatment strategy. I advise the reader to "ask your teacher" about doing some of these activities in the classroom. The sensory therapeutic experiences program, or STEP, to assist the student is commonly referred to as a "sensory diet" of experiences arranged by an occupational therapist, often in combination with other therapists, as well. I like to call it a "sensory banquet," because of the positive connotations of abundance, joy, and choice in that term. Please do what you can to support the sensory-avoiding student's sincere attempts to make life work in your classroom. This book provides dozens of suggestions for simple classroom activities and accommodations that, if done as described, also benefit classmates and relevant school personnel, as well as the student.

Sensory-banquet activities, however, are not the whole story. Toxic chemical exposures can interfere with brain functioning and worsen sensory-avoidance symptoms. *According to an ever-expanding wealth of scientific studies, it is especially important to guard against toxic exposures with students who are on the autism spectrum or who have attention-deficit disorder (with or without hyperactivity).* Guard air purity by using low-odor whiteboard markers or use a chalkboard. Have an electronic air purifier available at all times and ventilate with fresh air whenever feasible. Avoid air mists and room deodorizers and wearing perfume or cologne. Guard the purity of snacks and beverages by emphasizing protein-rich and additive-free foods and beverages, and provide constant convenient access to pure filtered water. *Sports drinks are never acceptable.* Provide a list of safe snacks as a handout for all parents. You can find excellent guidelines at *www.schools-lunch.org.*

In addition to hunting for opportunities to provide the sensory-banquet therapeutic activities, there is much you can do to facilitate the student's adjustment. A comprehensive video portrayal of these kinds of activities is The School Success Tool Kit, and my preferred book describing them is *Sensory Integration: Practical Strategies and Sensory Motor Activities for Use in the Classroom.* Both of these resources are described in the Resources section of this book.

Minimize sensory overload by placing furniture so that there is ample room for passing between and getting in and out of desks and chairs. Select desk locations with respect to possible distractions and consider offering two desks for the student—one in the large group setting and one in a quiet area.

A student with sensory issues is chaotic on the "inside" and needs constancy on the "outside." Keep processes routine, predictable, and orderly. Whenever you are teaching, "break it down and slow it down." Emphasize the bridging of concepts (connecting one to another) and introduce today's new material as a variation of yesterday's material. Post an easy-to-read schedule in the front of the room, and consider providing an additional schedule at the student's desk. Give ample notice in advance for any changes in routine.

Give a clear indication of all homework assignments and times due, both verbally and visually. Repeat instructions for the student as an aid to understanding. Give no more than two directions at a time, concisely, and teach by using one sensory modality at a time. Gain the student's attention before speaking and use clearly pronounced, concrete, and simple words (monosyllabic, if possible). Use small sentences without complex clauses. Give directives to the entire class whenever possible ("It's time for all of us to put our toys away," rather than "Put your toys away, Jason.").

Aid in transitions to calm-focus tasks by having the student stretch, twist, jump, pull, push, or walk around. Doing finger exercises or slight rocking on an inflated seat cushion might also help. Aid in transitions to writing tasks by having the student reach up and down, press palms together, pull on each finger, or squeeze something, such as a ball, some modeling compound, or a balloon filled with sand or rice.

Sensory avoiders are very easily bothered by distractions. Try to reduce, relocate, or eliminate visual and auditory distractions. The student might be bothered one day but not the next by any potentially bothersome stimuli. If the student is visually sensitive, control for glare by allowing the student to wear a visor or baseball cap and seat the student out of direct sunlight. If the student is bothered by fluorescent lighting (a common problem with visual avoiders), arrange to have an incandescent-bulb floor lamp with a shade.

To reduce auditory distraction, provide white noise in the classroom by using an aquarium filter, an air purifier, a fan, or music. I always advise "low, slow, and no" music: low volume, slow beat, and no drum. Reduce olfactory distraction by eliminating the source, seating the student far from the source, having fresh air ventilation, running an electric air purifier, and growing odor-absorbing plants as a science unit.

If the student seems to need some whole-body movement, you can arrange for it while the student is seated at his or her desk. Have the student squeeze the chair legs with his feet, make slight rocking movements, rub his feet on a small piece of carpet under the desk, sit on a small cushion, press in with his ankles against an ace bandage wrapped around the chair legs, or press forward with his feet against a bungee cord wrapped across the front legs of the chair.

If the student seems to need some hand and arm movement, show the student how to do chair push-ups with his hands flat on the seat, push his fists deep into pockets, or manipulate a soft cloth, some yarn, or a string you provide. Offering a clipboard to write on rather than using the desktop is sometimes helpful.

To help a sensory-avoiding student feel more grounded, provide a chair that allows the student's feet to be flat on the floor, provide a desk that is at belt level, avoid bucket-seat plastic chairs, install rubber tips on the legs of the student's chair and desk, and provide support to keep the student's torso upright. Provide gravitational input by letting the student wear a weighted vest or weighted belt dangles, hold a heavy book in his lap, or wear weighted anklets.

The child's number-one defense against stress is healthy self-esteem. Take advantage of the student's strong learning channels. Have the student explore a subject of special interest, and maintain a high ratio (90:10) of "success" to "challenge." Gradually increase the difficulty level of instructional material, giving the concrete, then the abstract; the simple, then the complex; the parts, then the connections between them; the easier, then the more difficult aspects.

Allow protective distance to prevent emotional overload by letting the student sit within structured separated spaces, like on an assigned carpet square during circle time or at the end of a table or at a separate desk, or in the first or last position when standing in line. Encourage self-care during stressful moments by designating a special place within your classroom with a catchy name, such as "Time-In Place," "Concentration Station," or "Take-A-Break Place." Equip it with such objects as a cushion, squeezable ball or yarn ball, squeezable toy animals, Teddy bear or other "companion," beanbag chair, pillow, blanket, or comforter.

Always be alert for any indication that the student is being too bothered or too distracted by sensory distortions. Work with the lead therapist (usually an occupational therapist) in deciding which of the many classroom suggestions and activities in this book to try. By making these simple adjustments, you can contribute greatly to classroom success for any student who is a sensory avoider.

# About the Author

*John F. Taylor, PhD,* is a pioneering authority on attention-deficit disorder (ADD), who has long championed the cause of better recognition of the sensory aspects of the disorder. His video DVD, The School Success Tool Kit, is the most comprehensive portrayal of classroom and home-based sensory accommodations available. The length of a motion picture, it depicts more than 125 no-cost techniques for use with children who have sensory issues, filmed in actual homes and classrooms. Among his many books are *The Survival Guide for Kids with ADD or ADHD; Diet, Toxins, ADHD and Behavior;* and *The Early Childhood Fun Express* (which he coauthored), featuring many sensory-friendly procedures for home and school use. John conducts seminars on Sensory Processing Disorder throughout the United States and has been featured on national interview shows. He can be reached through his Web site and online bookstore, *www.ADD-Plus.com.*

# About the Illustrator

Having left her executive marketing position in the Northeast, **Lynda Farrington Wilson** is enjoying an eclectic career pursuing her art through writing, illustrating, and throwing pottery in North Carolina. She recently authored and illustrated *Squirmy Wormy: How I Learned to Help Myself*, a children's book about coping with sensory issues. Lynda is certified in the Affect-based Language Curriculum and has created ArtFriends, a unique social skills class model providing sensory and social experiences through the arts. She and her husband have three sons, the youngest a funny, brilliant sensory-seeker with high-functioning autism.

# Additional Resources

**Sensory World**, a proud division of Future Horizons, is the world's largest publisher devoted exclusively to resources for those interested in Sensory Processing Disorder. They also sponsor national conferences for parents, teachers, therapists, and others interested in supporting those with Sensory Processing Disorder. Visit *www.sensoryworld.com* for further information.

Sensory World
1010 N Davis St • Arlington, TX 76012
Phone: (877) 775-8968 or (682) 558-8941
Fax: (682) 558-8945
*info@sensoryworld.com* • *www.sensoryworld.com*

Sensory products include: *Answers to Questions Teachers Ask About Sensory Integration, The Goodenoughs Get in Sync, The Sensory Connection, Prechool SENSE, Starting SI Therapy, MoveAbout Cards, 28 Instant Songames, Songames for Sensory Integration, Danceland, Marvelous Mouth Music, The Out-of-Sync Child* video, *Making Sense of Sensory Integration, Teachers Ask about Sensory Integration, Eyegames,* and *Soothing the Senses.*

**"Quiet Time"** is a 15-minute audio relaxation CD available from *www.ADD-Plus.com*. It is the only relaxation CD that has a money-back guarantee to calm any child between the ages of 5 and 11.

# Index